T0222179

AI FOR CREATIVITY

AI FOR EVERYTHING

Artificial intelligence (AI) is all around us. From driverless cars to game-winning computers to fraud protection, AI is already involved in many aspects of life, and its impact will only continue to grow in future. Many of the world's most valuable companies are investing heavily in AI research and development, and not a day goes by without news of cutting-edge breakthroughs in AI and robotics.

The *AI for Everything* series will explore the role of AI in contemporary life, from cars and aircraft to medicine, education, fashion, and beyond. Concise and accessible, each book is written by an expert in the field and will bring the study and reality of AI to a broad readership including interested professionals, students, researchers, and lay readers.

AI for Immunology
Louis J. Catania

AI for Cars
Hanky Sjafrie & Josep Aulinas

AI for Digital Warfare
Niklas Hageback & Daniel Hedblom

AI for Art
Niklas Hageback & Daniel Hedblom

AI for Creativity
Niklas Hageback

AI for Death and Dying
Maggi Savin-Baden

AI for Radiology
Oge Marques

AI for Games
Ian Millington

AI for School Teachers
Rose Luckin & Karine George

AI for Learners
Carmel Kent, Benedict du Boulay & Rose Luckin

AI for Social Justice
Alan Dix and Clara Crivellaro

For more information about this series please visit:
https://www.routledge.com/AI-for-Everything/book-series/AIFE

AI FOR CREATIVITY

NIKLAS HAGEBACK

CRC Press
Taylor & Francis Group
Boca Raton London New York

CRC Press is an imprint of the
Taylor & Francis Group, an **informa** business

First Edition published 2022
by CRC Press
6000 Broken Sound Parkway NW, Suite 300, Boca Raton, FL 33487-2742

and by CRC Press
2 Park Square, Milton Park, Abingdon, Oxon, OX14 4RN

© 2022 Niklas Hageback

CRC Press is an imprint of Taylor & Francis Group, LLC

Library of Congress Cataloging-in-Publication Data
Names: Hageback, Niklas, author.
Title: AI for creativity / Niklas Hageback.
Description: First edition. | Boca Raton: CRC Press, 2022. |
Series: AI for everything | Includes bibliographical references and index.
Identifiers: LCCN 2021019342 | ISBN 9781032048673 (hardback) |
ISBN 9781032047751 (paperback) | ISBN 9781003194941 (ebook)
Subjects: LCSH: Computational intelligence. | Artificial intelligence. | Creative ability.
Classification: LCC Q342 .H34 2022 | DDC 006.3—dc23
LC record available at https://lccn.loc.gov/2021019342

ISBN: 978-1-032-04867-3 (hbk)
ISBN: 978-1-032-04775-1 (pbk)
ISBN: 978-1-003-19494-1 (ebk)

DOI: 10.1201/9781003194941

Typeset in Joanna
by codeMantra

CONTENTS

Author   vii

Introduction   1

1   The Creative Process   5

2   The Creative Enigma   19

3   Perspectives on Creativity   41

4   Computational Creativity   69

References   89
Index   97

AUTHOR

Niklas Hageback has an extensive background in digital transformations and risk management. He has held regional executive management and project oversight roles at leading banks, including Credit Suisse, Deutsche Bank, and Goldman Sachs, in both Asia and Europe, where he was in charge of a number of complex regionwide digital transformation and risk management initiatives. More recently, he has done extensive work in Artificial Intelligence, notably machine learning, leading the development of automated human reasoning and computational creativity applications. He is a published author with bestsellers including *The Mystery of Market Movements: An Archetypal Approach to Investment Forecasting and Modelling* (2014), *The Virtual Mind: Designing the Logic to Approximate Human Thinking* (2017), *The Death Drive: Why Societies Self-Destruct* (2020), and *Leadership in The Digital Age: Renaissance of The Renaissance Man* (2020). He has also published a number of research papers in AI and finance.

INTRODUCTION

Every discovery contains an irrational element or a creative intuition.

Karl Popper, Austro-British philosopher (1902–1994),
The Logic of Scientific Discovery

One of the most notable features that makes us humans a distinctly unique species is our creative capacity providing, at times, an *extraordinary* productivity and remarkable innovations, an ability that through quantum leap innovations has propelled us to the current digital age. However, generating creative breakthroughs are easier said than done, they appear less frequent and in a more scattered manner than desired, it seems that we have not yet fully cracked the creative code, allowing us to advance academia, commerce, and science entirely at our will. There is a puzzling irrational element to it which makes creativity hard to control, much to the dismay of authoritarian regimes, and as history has shown, it is not always easy to produce the expected results to solve elusive problems, and when breakthroughs do come, they tend to carry the hallmarks of serendipity. A lot of research has been put into understanding the creative process, given the great value it holds both commercially and intellectually, but the mechanism behind our creative capabilities has proven stubbornly difficult to explain. The critical junction of creative breakthroughs which often come through so-called *Eureka* moments, its activation and origin remain enigmatic, and deliberately trying to provoke it into action has often proven futile.

DOI: 10.1201/9781003194941-1

However, artificial intelligence with its aspiration to replicate the human mind is set to change all that. Key areas of artificial intelligence have been progressing remarkably swift and now allow for no longer only envisaging computational creativity as a future aspiration but actually embarking on the practical work with the design and development of tools that can be embedded into the human creative process. The integration between the human mind and its artificial counterpart is thereby perhaps nearing its completion. But what will that look like and will it be the missing link in the quest for a seamless man–machine interconnectivity?

AI for Creativity is a book for anyone with an interest in the advancement of artificial intelligence, notably the truly fascinating prospect of computational creativity. By being guided on how the human creative process works, the reader is equipped with an understanding of the design principles of the ongoing research and work on various applications that aspires to empower artificially induced creativity. The book provides a fascinating read of what is currently emerging in a truly cutting-edge area of artificial intelligence, how tools are being developed to enable computational creativity that holds the propensity to dramatically change our lives.

The book is structured in four chapters that detail the creative process and what has been ascertained about it. It also makes a deep dive into the enigmatic part of creativity that borders almost to the mystical and provides a plethora of perspectives on creativity from art to science. The book explains the in-depth conceptual sketch on what computational creativity might look like and how it is set to operate, and finally, it concludes with highlights of how the holistic man–machine connect is about to accelerate human creativity into an unprecedented phase.

CHAPTER 1: THE CREATIVE PROCESS

The creative process has been a vital part of human development where ingenious albeit highly uncertain ventures have been able to advance and improve our lives considerably. The importance of creativity was early on recognised and how it unfolds has intrigued many, given the great both commercial and intellectual values it holds. Something that has proven easier said than done, as creativity appears hard to provoke into action and put on a desired trajectory, there is an element of irrationality over the whole process that is difficult to bring under control and ensure that it unleashes at will. However, with Graham Wallas' theories about a century ago, we got a first structural overview of the creative process with what ensuing steps it required as well as a method to ascertain it. What did that look like and where are we now, do we understand creativity any better than a century ago?

CHAPTER 2: THE CREATIVE ENIGMA

Already in the Classical Era, observations were made of creative individuals' often peculiar behaviour, not unusually bordering towards madness, and sometimes even crossing that border. Then as now, it was hard to pin down the source and mechanism behind the sudden ingenious sparks that triggered the creation of artistic masterpieces by these eccentric individuals. It came, perhaps as a lack of better explanations, to be associated with divine forces, as it was simply too irrational to be possible to define in rational terms. What did that look like and how does it compare to how we understand creativity today? In a sense, we have not advanced that much further today: this out-of-a-blue serendipitous insight, described as a revelation with an elevation of understanding of sorts, remains something of an enigma. What are the current hypotheses on the origin and advent of this sudden enlightenment, and can we distinguish any common red threads throughout history when seeking to explain the source of creativity?

CHAPTER 3: PERSPECTIVES ON CREATIVITY

Obviously, creativity is applied in many disciplines from art to science and perhaps as a surprise to many even in religion. By taking a stab on how it has been described and fathomed from these many perspectives and cross-referencing these, interestingly, common denominators emerge. Does that mean that there exists a generic creative process, agnostic of domains but requiring a subject matter expertise in order to fully capitalise on it?

CHAPTER 4: COMPUTATIONAL CREATIVITY

With a holistic understanding of the creative process, and in particular the phase where new illuminating insights occur, one can embark on articulating it through a conceptually designed blueprint which lends itself to a platform for application development in the area of computational creativity. With recent advances in artificial intelligence, including machine learning, we might just now have the tools to develop applications that will augment and facilitate the human cognitive process and eventually supersede it. This is an endeavour where artificial intelligence is truly put to test by trying to emulate the human mind's finest and most treasured faculty, our ability to create.

1

THE CREATIVE PROCESS

Creativity is a yearning for immortality.

Rollo May, American psychologist (1909–1994),
The Courage to Create (1975), p. 27

One of mankind's most important traits, the ability to innovate, has taken us from the brutal lives in caves to the modern-day digital era, and compared with other primates, creativity appears to be a defining characteristic for the human species. History provides us with the insights that human advances often happen through innovative jumps; quantum leap technological breakthroughs that have elevated our civilisation, from the discovery of fire, applying wheels for transportation, up to the splitting of atoms and beyond, of the former we know little of the creative process, of the latter a lot, at least at the superficial level.

According to legend, it was when the Greek universal genius Archimedes stepped into the bathtub and noticed how the water levels raised, a sudden insight came over him on how to calculate volume, proclaiming Eureka! (I have found it!). Or when a falling apple provided the cue to the English physicist Isaac Newton that allowed him to formulate the laws of gravity. Or the German-American physicist Albert Einstein's imaginary vision of riding on a beam of light that allegedly played a significant role in his development

DOI: 10.1201/9781003194941-2

of the *General Theory of Relativity*. And whilst some of these historical accounts are claimed to be, in parts at least, of a fictitious nature, the phenomena they highlight are not.

The process of creativity has been closely linked with these *Eureka* moments: sudden cognitive breakthroughs that, whilst being rare, unfold a previously unthought perspective and provide annotative knowledge surpassing the existing scientific doctrine. They allow for paradigm shifts of the thought narrative. Sometimes, it carries the traits of the aforementioned sudden revelation of sorts; at other times, it is part of a more gradual process where the levels of insight advance step by step. "Thinking outside the box" plays an important role as part of the ability to view the world differently than contemporary scientists, but not just in a random manner. This is also a madman's worldview that differs from the normative perspective, yet he does not manage to proceed beyond disarray, whilst the truly innovative individual, in contrast, manages to out of the chaotic find order that delivers new insights and augment our understanding of certain phenomena. However, creativity as manifested in innovative achievements and the great arts seems bestowed only a few. It appears that creativity, of such highly abstract calibre at least, must be viewed as an add-on to what can be defined as "normal" human thought patterns. This is highlighted from the recognition that a considerable number of innovations originate from the so-called lonely genius, characterised through a combination of obsessively hard work, the courage to see things through against the reigning, often hostile, convictions, and the ability to view the world through a distinctly different spectrum. What sets the genius apart is that what appears to be a chaotic chasm in the process of creativity to the layman is where he through a structured process, albeit the innovator himself generally is at pain of explaining it, often manages to produce new valuable insights. Domain expertise plays a key role in designated creativity taking into account a well-organised knowledge base, much as the mathematician needs specific tools to solve mathematical problems, something which the layman lacks. Creativity in that sense assumes a certain level of expertise: a mathematical illiterate will not, if ever, be able to understand and explore mathematical concepts and then identify creative solutions. However, domain expertise carries a danger; in it lie tacit assumptions that can become cognitive chains that are being taken for granted, and it thus becomes hard to detach oneself from intellectually as they serve as edificial axioms.

By exploring various innovative exhibits, it provides us with a better understanding of the human mind and why its breakthrough creative manifests appear so relatively few and far between. To start with, a crisp definition of the word "creative" is needed; such as it being an intelligible, whilst unorthodox and by the standards of the day even bizarre, manner of approaching a situation or a problem, and arriving at a previously unthought value adding solution. The mysterious part of this process, which will be explained in detail further on, is when creativity calls upon factors not seemingly accessible to our rational thought process, structured through some sorting mechanism where in hindsight the solution often appears to always have lingered on, it is just that there and then everything comes together, and it becomes the proverbial eye opener. In essence, to understand creativity is to understand the importance of a relatively rare and elevated human condition, with the view that what one can understand, one can also attempt to model, which is the main purpose of this book.

THE HISTORICAL PERSPECTIVE

Creativity was early on associated with divine inspiration conferred through the mercy of God, a privilege for only certain entitled individuals who were provided a gift of grace that brought insights to what was considered to be hidden knowledge. Thus, sudden revelations were considered externally induced with humans acting as agents temporarily equipped with divine wisdom. The Greek philosopher Plato (428/427 or 424/423–348/347 BC) argued that creativity was also influencing poets and artists, receiving inspiration from non-human sources, and that their artworks were therefore really God's creations and not the artists. Creativity of the level that it could render artistic masterpieces was viewed to be distributed through divine favouritism and therefore not something that humans could ignite themselves through extensive training.[1,2]

At the moment of inspiration, it was considered that the rational personality subsided, and emotions overcome the artist that were applied to elaborate on his fantasies, and often it was a highly subjective experience that transcended both time and space. This celestial aspect is not only found within Christianity but is a domain that exists in many religions and is not always regarded as positive, where elements of ecstasy and mysticism, sometimes regarded as delusional, have been noted. It was, however, first during the *Renaissance* that creativity started to be viewed as a human faculty coming from within rather than outside, and it was regarded as one of the specific characteristics of the human genius, the Italian polymath Leonardo da Vinci (1452–1519) being a case in point, as individuals with multitalented capabilities. This more human-centric outlook of the world, playing down the influence of divine forces came in the 18th century further in the forefront, and the links between imagination and creativity were highlighted, coinciding with the *Age of Enlightenment*, as well as the connection with levels of cognitive ability. Science was then also able to make a separation in the levels of intelligence, enabled through the first methodological research and the introduction of IQ tests which could distinguish between talent, high intelligence, and genius, where creativity was largely seen as a characteristic of the latter but not the former.[3,4,5]

GRAHAM WALLAS

One of the first systematic studies of the process of creativity was that of the English psychologist Graham Wallas (1858–1932). In his book from 1926, *The Art of Thought*, Walls identified four stages of creativity:

1 preparation;
2 incubation;
3 illumination; and
4 verification.[6]

As part of the preparation phase, the problem, or issue, at hand is detailed and defined, and the data and information required are collated and categorised. The background material is analysed, and a knowledge base is being accumulated. The preparation phase also entails the planning of the project.

Differing from the preparation, which is a consciously active and deliberate phase, during the incubation phase, much of the problem-solving activity is conducted in an unconscious manner. This is in a sense the most mysterious part of the whole process, where the conscious consideration of the problem is replaced by unconscious contemplation in which Boolean logic is relaxed, and association-based thought processes, also of the bizarre kind, are engaged. In Wallas' own words:

> Voluntary abstention from conscious thought on any problem may, itself, take two forms: the period of abstention may be spent either in conscious mental work on other problems, or in a relaxation from all conscious mental work. The first kind of Incubation economizes time, and is therefore often the better.[7]

This incubation phase often comes with a great deal of frustration and anxiety, in that usually large numbers of proposed ideas prove futile. The emotional stress that builds up brings further coercion on the unconscious mental processes. Obviously, a lot of research projects end at the incubation phase, as they fail to find a workable solution, but in some instances, a creative idea out of the chaos, or simply void, arises. Some describe the incubation phase as that the characteristics of the problem are hypothesised into an abstract mental representation and then are tweaked, distorted, and rearranged in various manners in the unconscious part of the mind, and at best resurfaced into awareness as a viable solution.

The arrival of the solution, the Eureka moment, represents the third phase of Wallas' model, the illumination phase. It cannot directly be consciously forced or provoked to conclusion, but a solution is largely dictated by the unconscious' ability to form variations of the mental model representing the problem. Once a solution has emerged, it needs validation, and to formulate the often highly symbolic vision into proper prose and mathematics, much like Einstein transformed his vision of riding a lightning beam into the general theory of relativity. This is manifested in *the verification phase*.[8]

THE VARIOUS FACETS OF CREATIVITY

Creativity is typically defined as the capability to generate ideas or develop new products and services that are original in character and (economically) valuable. Considering the potential financial benefits, creativity is not only a topic for psychology and cognitive science, but also for economics, business studies, and education, given the game-changing value that it can bring to business and industry, and the study thereof has also expanded into engineering and artificial intelligence. Thus, introducing the fostering of creativity in the educational system and at workplaces has become a key ingredient in the knowledge-based economy which has come to depend on continuous innovation for growth and prosperity. Most researchers agree that certain cognitive components are necessary for creativity, including the capability to make flexible associations between abstract thoughts and the capacity to generate original ideas that are apt to the task at hand, as simply unusual ideas that are not useful or adaptive should not be considered creative.[9,10,11]

However, intellectual capabilities are not enough for creativity, it also requires a personality that is willing to confront conformity, in other words a certain courageous, even rebellious, streak. To this there needs to be a willingness to deal with great uncertainties, as it is typically associated with engaging in work lacking defined output, even paths to solutions, and thus involves considerable risk-taking, features known only to motivate certain individuals. And to no surprise, studies highlight that individuals with an inherent curiosity tend to be more motivated for engaging in creative type of work.[12,13,14]

Conformist societies tend to maintain one single interpretation of reality, to the extent of being dogmatic, but creativity, independent of domain, requires going beyond and challenging the prescribed conventional wisdoms. The creative, risk-seeking personality is sometimes connected with transgressions, as creativity can be viewed as a break with the existing rules and defining new ways of doing things, at times in stark contrast with the existing methods and perceived truths. Pablo Picasso's comment that "every act of creation is first of all an act of destruction" is therefore to the point. Some philosophical studies have shown a linkage between creativity and dishonesty, traits working in both directions; creativity may lead to dishonesty, and vice versa, dishonesty may lead to creativity, and creative people have in studies shown to be more likely to bend rules and even break laws.[15,16,17] Whilst this might be a peculiar observation and obviously disturbing from an ethical perspective, the term "thinking outside the box" should therefore be loosely equated with "thinking outside the rules".[18,19,20] So, creative thinking typically requires that one break some, but maybe not all, rules within a expertise domain to allow for and construct associations between previously unconnected elements.[21,22] The resulting unusual mental conjunctions then serve as the basis for exploring and elaborating novel ideas.[23,24]

THERE IS CREATIVITY AND THEN THERE IS CREATIVITY...

One can distinguish between primary (sometimes labelled major) and secondary (or minor) creativity, where primary creativity represents something uniquely new, in effect a paradigm shift, and secondary creativity consists of new innovative ways of applying an already-known technology, for instance. The creativity researcher Margret A. Boden distinguishes between three types of creativity: combinational (the unfamiliar combinations of familiar ideas); exploratory (exploring a conceptual space); and the most radical kind of creativity, transformational (transforming a conceptual space), the enabling of thoughts that have not been thought before.[25] Hence, there are different ways of characterising creativity, and various proponents argue their type of classifications, but broadly they fall within two main conduits: the breakthrough paradigm shifting type and the deployment of existing methods in a new value-adding manner.

Related to creativity is the concept of *imagination*, or fantasies, the ability to produce abstract images and ideas in the mind without the need to deploy any immediate input from the senses. It is a cognitive process that can be beneficial in the problem-solving process but cannot be equalised to creativity. The difference lies in purpose as creativity is required to produce something valuable, aiming for the tangible, often but not always translated into monetary terms, whilst imagination typically does not progress beyond (the enjoyment of) the produced image or object itself. Whereas creative solutions require deliberate efforts, imagination can flow more spontaneously and playfully without any specific directions. Imagination functions more in the way of directionless daydreaming where thoughts are mostly randomly wandering, sometimes however being elaborated into a highly complex fantasy world. Qualitatively therefore both concepts can be on equal footing, as imaginations can be almost painstakingly crafted out into minutiae details and in imagination lies often also the improbable. Imagination does hold useful properties as it relaxes norms, conventions, and boundaries, and exercises such as targeted experimental imaginations and guided brainstorming sessions can serve the purpose of creativity; hence, imagination is a vital part of the creative process.

CREATIVITY'S CLOSE COUSINS

Given that creativity has been studied from various facets of psychology, often with individual psychologists, or others, labelling similar concepts with their own jargon, it is of interest to draw in these as reference points to broaden the understanding of creativity and the psychological environments and settings where it can be nurtured.

FLOW

The American psychologist Mihály Csíkszentmihályi introduced the concept of *flow*, occasionally being referred to as *being in the zone*, indicating a mental state in which an individual is so focused on a task with all his energy going into it, that the world around is fading out due to the dedicated absorption in what one does, losing sense of both space and time. Whilst the phenomena have long been known, under other names, notable as meditation techniques in certain Eastern religions, Csíkszentmihályi applied flow generically. In flow, as all energy is focused on the task at hand, the isolation facilitates the concentration efforts helping to augment the idea generation process, amongst others.[26]

Csikszentmihalyi, in addition on how creativity can be facilitated through flow, also proposed that its characteristics can be compared with the evolutionary process through its interaction between the components: *variation*, *selection*, and *transmission*. Using this framework, he argued that creativity becomes a sort of mutation, where the many variations that by its contemporary are ranked through their survivability and adaptability. Only the creative ideas meeting these criteria will be considered value adding and selected with a view of being popularised and adapted into ways of doing things. He deploys the term *memes* to explain how creative value-adding ideas are introduced, transmitted, and embedded in the existing cultures. This interaction is promoted through three concepts: first one being *area*, considered to be a sub-group of culture. Area consists of a collection of memes in regulated contexts in which the structure becomes the prerequisite to store information, and as such, it remains available for future references. The second element is the *individual*, whose contribution in the creative process consists of extracting information from the area and producing variations thereof. The third element evaluates these proposals, namely *expertise*. The transmission of successful creative ideas in society is promoted through the acknowledgement by these three groups.[27]

THE THREE SISTERS OF THINKING – DIVERGENT/CONVERGENT/LATERAL

Divergent thinking is considered to be an ability to formulate a number of answers to a problem, of which some of them could be considered unique or original. To that point, tests have been crafted, such as coming up with as many potential use areas as possible for a paper clip, a brick, etc. As per the design of such a test, divergent thinking is defined as occurring spontaneously and in a free-flowing fashion, often under time pressure and seeking to promote unexpected connections.

Convergent thinking, on the other hand, is structured by following a particular set of logical steps in order to arrive to what hopefully will be a productive solution. Hence, divergent and convergent thinking can work in ensuing steps, such as a brainstorming session representing divergent thinking producing a plethora of ideas, and once that has been concluded, convergent thinking assists in structuring and organising these ideas with a view of seeking out the one(s) most value adding.

Lateral thinking is another approach to problem-solving where the unexpected is applied, often by introducing humorous elements, such as word plays, with the ambition of bringing new insights to a problem that hopefully delivers a beneficial solution. This kind of surprise style thought patterns is applied to identify new thought combinations previously not appearing obvious. All these exercises seek to enhance the environment in which creativity can be spurred, and rather than involving incubation phases with its uncontrollable unconscious element, instead they aim to engage conscious proactive methodologies. There is a strong emphasis of breaking thought blocks and routine stereotypical thinking, in which humour often plays an important role in providing absurdity, even slightly mad perspectives. And there might be something to these thought games, as streaks of madness which we will see in the next chapter appear to link to creative capabilities.[28]

CONCLUSIONS

Creativity includes an element of transgression which means previous thought patterns and preconceived notions are challenged, eventually disregarded, and a new thought paradigm comes to rule our narrative. The jury is out on how the creative spark ignites, but it appears to carry some unconscious tenets, as even the conscious-only proponents are at a loss to fully model the identification of suitable solutions. Instead, associative-based thinking that somehow is actively searching for solutions carrying harmonious aestheticism appears to be at work and is largely happening beyond our active control. The capacity for being able to generate highly abstract creative solutions requires not only domain expertise but also a sufficiently high cognitive level which explains why despite so many governmental efforts around the world to promote creativity, there still are so relatively few successful innovation and entrepreneurial centres.

NOTES

1 Plato. *The Republic of Plato Vol. 2 Books VI-X* (Cambridge Library Collection – Classics, Cambridge: Cambridge University Press, Reissue edition, 2010).

2 Rothenberg, Albert & Hausman, Carl R. *The Creativity Question* (Durham, NC: Duke University Press Books, 1976).

3 Albert, R. S. & Runco, M. A. A History of Research on Creativity. (In R. J. Sternberg (Ed.), *Handbook of Creativity*, Cambridge: Cambridge University Press, 1999), p. 5.

4 Niu, Weihua & Sternberg, Robert J. The Philosophical Roots of Western and Eastern Conceptions of Creativity *(Journal of Theoretical and Philosophical Psychology*, 26(1–2), 2006), pp. 18–38.

5 Library of Congress. *Rome Reborn: The Vatican Library & Renaissance Culture.* https://www.loc.gov/exhibits/vatican/humanism.html (accessed 1 April 2021).

6 Wallas, Graham. *The Art of Thought* (Kent, England: Solis Press, 2014 edition, original 1926).

7 Ibid.

8 Ibid.

9 Sternberg, R. J. & Lubart, T. I. Investing in Creativity (*American Psychologist*, 51(7), 1996), pp. 677–688.

10 Lubart, T. I. Creativity (In R. J. Sternberg (Ed.), *Thinking and Problem Solving*, San Diego, CA: Academic, 1994), pp. 290–332.

11 Ochse, R. *Before the Gates of Excellence: The Determinants of Creative Genius* (New York: Cambridge University Press, 1990).

12 Sternberg, R. J. & Lubart, T. I. Investing in Creativity (*American Psychologist*, 51(7), 1996), pp. 677–688.

13 Lubart, T. I. Creativity (In R. J. Sternberg (Ed.), *Thinking and Problem Solving*, San Diego, CA: Academic, 1994), pp. 290–332.

14 Ochse, R. *Before the Gates of Excellence: The Determinants of Creative Genius* (New York: Cambridge University Press, 1990).

15 Cropley, D. H., Kaufman, J. C., & Cropley, A. J. Malevolent Creativity: A Functional Model of Creativity in Terrorism and Crime (*Creativity Research Journal*, 20, April 2008), pp. 105–115.

16 Sulloway, F. J. *Born to Rebel: Birth Order, Family Dynamics, and Creative Lives* (New York: Pantheon Books, 1996).

17 Gino, Francesca & Wiltermuth, Scott S. Evil Genius? How Dishonesty Can Lead to Greater Creativity (*Psychological Science*, 25, February 18, 2014), pp. 973–981.

18 Guilford, J. P. Creativity: Yesterday, Today and Tomorrow (*Journal of Creative Behavior*, 1, Winter 1967), pp. 3–14.

19 Runco, M. A. Divergent Thinking, Creativity, and Ideation (In J. C. Kaufman & R. J. Sternberg (Eds.), *The Cambridge Handbook of Creativity*, New York: Cambridge University Press, 2010), pp. 413–446.

20 Simonton, Dean Keith. Creativity as Blind Variation and Selective Retention: Is the Creative Process Darwinian? (*Psychological Inquiry*, 10(4), 1999), pp. 309–328.

21 Bailin, Sharon. Critical and Creative Thinking (*Informal Logic*, 9(1), 1987), pp. 23–30.

22 Guilford, J. P. Creativity (*American Psychologist*, 5(9), 1950), pp. 444–454.

23 Langley, P. & Jones, R. A Computational Model of Scientific Insight (In R. J. Sternberg (Ed.), *The Nature of Creativity: Contemporary Psychological Perspectives*, Cambridge: Cambridge University Press, 1988), pp. 177–201.

24 Sternberg, R. J. A Triangular Theory of Love (*Psychological Review*, 93, 1986), pp. 119–135.

25 Boden, Margret, A. *The Creative Mind: Myths and Mechanisms* (London, UK: Routledge, 2004).

26 Csikszentmihályi, Mihaly. *Flow: The Psychology of Optimal Experience* (New York: Harper & Row, 1990).

27 Csikszentmihályi, Mihaly. *Handbook of Creativity* (Edited extract from R. Sternberg (Ed.), Cambridge: Cambridge University Press, 1990), pp. 313–335.

28 De Bono, Edward. *Lateral Thinking: Creativity Step by Step* (New York: Harper & Row, 1970).

2

THE CREATIVE ENIGMA

The chief enemy of creativity is good sense
                    Pablo Picasso, Spanish artist (1881–1973)

WHERE DOES CREATIVITY COME FROM?
VARIOUS THEORIES

Most theories on the creative process either focus on the high-level decomposition of the various phases, much like Wallas' hypothesis as previously described, or aim at only specific stages of the process, typically the incubation phase, which to date remains the least understood. The latter theories are, however, mostly incomplete due to their constrained objectives and are often incompatible with each other, sometimes because of the lack of standardised definitions of key concepts.

The reigning structural framework of scientific discovery was introduced by the American physicist Thomas Kuhn (1922–1996) in his 1962 book *The Structure of Scientific Revolutions* in which he suggested that scientific knowledge, rather than following a path of linear progress, advances through infrequent spurts of knowledge jumps or paradigm shifts. This new set of knowledge is being recognised as a scientific truth by the research community, and there is obviously a subjective element in this acknowledgement, but it will set the axioms that

DOI: 10.1201/9781003194941-3

going forward dictate the interpretation of ensuing scientific findings. As history has highlighted, these paradigm shifts often have their roots in the sudden eureka moments as part of the process of creativity and fit well as the catalyst of paradigm shifts, albeit not exclusively intended as such. However, whilst Kuhn presented a framework of scientific progress, he never was able to articulate how in practical terms creativity produced the innovations that triggered them.[1]

MASLOW ET AL.'S VIEW ON CREATIVITY

In contrast to Wallas' view on creativity stood the perspectives of the American psychologist Abraham Maslow (1908–1970), who is most famous for his "hierarchy of needs", a theory of the various priorities a human need to fulfil to aspire towards self-actualisation, a somewhat elusive term broadly meaning achieving one's full potential. This hierarchy consists of six steps, starting with the necessity for basic survival, such as having air to breath, food to eat, and water to drink, leading up to self-esteem and being free from any mental disturbances, eventually and hopefully arriving at the final step, self-actualisation, in which humans are comfortable enough to express themselves in a creative manner. Indeed, a different to "necessity is the mother to invention" or as a psychological mechanism to handle repressed perceptions. But Maslow argued that environment is not an important factor in the creative process, this as if a person has been able to meet self-actualisation, they can as part of reaching their full potential choose to be creative. Maslow saw creativity as a central feature to our personal growth, which would help us advance and live meaningful individual lives rather than just being one in the crowd. He splits creativity into three different types: primary, secondary, and integrated. With primary creativity, he referred to creative techniques that allowed us to cope in the everyday and get relief from stress, this would typically include creative art, like drawing, writing prose, painting, and so on. Maslow viewed this as a more spontaneous form of creativity. The secondary creativity is more intellectually demanding to aspire to, as it requires deliberate thought and planning prior to commencing its manifestations. Integrated creativity amalgamates primary and secondary creativity, out of it comes the great art, philosophy, and scientific landmarks. It is the pinnacle of innovative efforts of the self-actualised human being. It somewhat concurs with the Swiss psychologist Carl Gustav Jung's (1875–1961) view of visionary art. To Jung, these were superhuman creative efforts, somehow transcending beyond our conscious contemplation and comprehension. Broadening this perspective, the Austrian psychologist Alfred Adler (1870–1937) argued not only the importance of creativity as part of children's development, but also as a mean to handle various fears, such as death, and through one's creative manifestations somehow immortalising oneself, much in accordance with the reproductive instinct.[2,3]

Whilst the various perspectives point to different motivating powers to creativity, thus answering the why's however largely leaving the how's aside, most of these identified the incubation process as the mysterious part, where the inexplicable enlightenment took place, so exploring what we know about the incubation phase will help us gain an understanding on how to structure a computable model able of replicating and igniting creative sparks.

INCUBATION

The moment of sudden revelation where the worked-on problem is seen in a new light with a solution appearing is often labelled through the sometimes interchangeably used terms *intuition* and *insight*. The relationship between intuition and insight provides an interesting distinction in the understanding of the incubation phase. Some studies propose that intuition can be described through a continuous process based on experience but that insights are a discontinuous process.[4] Hence, they differ in that intuition is drawn from previous experiences, through learning and by gathering information from memory of a previous event or situation that shares certain similarities with current conditions. In essence, intuition is built on generalisations, making educated guesses based on probabilities, and if well developed, these are being correct enough to improve our capacity to forecast and handle unknown situations. So, intuition functions as a decision-making and problem-solving aid when the required information and causal analysis of the situation at hand are (temporarily) unavailable. Thus, intuition can be defined as:

> the power of the mind by which it immediately perceives the truth of things without reasoning or analysis; a truth so perceived, immediate, instinctive knowledge or belief.[5]

What the definition implicitly highlights is that intuition makes no attempt to provide causality, the understanding will have to come later and be deliberately sought after, in here lies an element of uncontrollability, making intuition difficult to be proactively evoked, rather appearing spontaneously and instantaneously, which on the other hand makes it hard to ignore.[6] It is important to realise that intuition must release a signal of sorts that is strong enough to trigger the urge to recognise it.[7] As intuition originates from the unconscious part of our minds, it hence explains it being beyond our capacity to control, something which also includes the gathering of perceptions and pattern-recognising activities that are conducted below our level of awareness. It is by some referred to as knowing without knowing why.[8] It can therefore be understood as an unconscious process, which provides a hunch allowing to make a judgement, often endorsed by a positive affective state described as a gut feeling.[9,10,11]

Complementing intuition, insight can therefore be defined as:

> the recognition of new connections across existing knowledge.[12]

Similar to intuition, insights also appear as a sudden revelation with an unconscious origin. It is thus a sort of tacit knowledge, and it takes the form of a mental shift that allows for viewing the components of a problem in a new light, producing a suggested solution.[13]

CREATIVITY AND THE UNCONSCIOUS

As according to most theories, the critical phase of the creative breakthrough appears to emanate from the unconscious, the question then arises; what is it in the unconscious that occurs that the conscious are not capable of doing?

More up-to-date research has pointed out the role the unconscious play for both idea generation and idea selection. In one study, participants were requested to generate creative ideas, one group immediately after deliberate consideration, and another group was allowed a period of unconscious contemplation. After noting down their ideas, the participants were asked to select the ones they viewed being the most creative. The performance in idea generation was considered similar between conscious and unconscious thought groups. However, the individuals in the unconscious thought group were ranked as better in selecting the most creative ideas. The research argued this as support for the theory that unconscious processes actively contribute to creativity, as it is unlikely that these findings are the exclusive consequence of set shifting or relaxation. The research suggests that unconscious processing is more adept at associating and integrating information than conscious processing is. Currently, the main debate between the advocates for different theories is whether during an incubation period, the unconscious processes contribute to creative thinking or whether it is merely the temporary absence of conscious thought that drives creativity. Traditionally, the incubation effect refers to the view that setting a problem aside for a while helps stimulating creative thought and problem-solving, as unconscious processes are working on the problem while the individual is not consciously thinking about it.[14,15] To this point, sometimes old and for the situation inappropriate ideas can cause mental fixation, impeding the generation of new and more valid ideas. Therefore, in addition to relaxing logic constraints and facilitating cues, it is argued that incubation effects can lead to the forgetting of fixating (unhelpful) elements and to mental set shifting, as the wrong cues become less accessible and instead provide a fresh, new, and unbiased starting point.[16,17]

The French mathematician Henri Poincaré (1854–1912) was among the first to explicitly write about this idea and solution-generating process, and naturally his focus was on mathematical creativity. He argued that trial and error played a key part in creativity, the production of random scenarios that contained various associations of ideas and elements which at times could give rise to solutions. However, given the almost infinite numbers of scenarios that can be conceived, how was the selection of the potentially useful ones conducted, and how were these brought forward to the conscious part of the mind for contemplation and evaluation? To Poincaré, it was hard to see how rules for this selection could be applied mechanically, he argued that they had to be felt rather than formulated. As this was done unconsciously and obviously beyond our deliberate control, Poincaré concluded that the unconscious must have an ability to perform a quality assessment of an idea's solution potential that the conscious part of the mind clearly was lacking. So, how does then a promising solution to a problem surface at the conscious level? Poincaré responded that it must from the intellectual point of view hold an aesthetic value, identified through expert insight in the domain area in question, so that a mathematician like himself would identify and feel the elegant quality of the proposed mathematical solution, whereas it would not appear obvious to a non-mathematician.[18]

To Albert Einstein, it was also clear that an unconscious element played a role in his associative thinking and highlighted that his thought process was expressed more often in pictures, he was quoted to say:

> I very rarely think in words at all. A thought comes, and I may try to express it in words afterward.[19]

To him, the appearance of a novel and lucid picture could be the solution to a problem. In 1945, he described this in a letter, as a response to a survey conducted on how scientists think:

My Dear Colleague:

In the following, I am trying to answer in brief your questions as well as I am able. I am not satisfied myself with those answers and I am willing to answer more questions if you believe this could be of any advantage for the very interesting and difficult work you have undertaken.

(A) The words or the language, as they are written or spoken, do not seem to play any role in my mechanism of thought. The psychical entities which seem to serve as elements in thought are certain signs and more or less clear images which can be "voluntarily" reproduced and combined.

There is, of course, a certain connection between those elements and relevant logical concepts. It is also clear that the desire to arrive finally at logically connected concepts is the emotional basis of this rather vague play with the above-mentioned elements. But taken from a psychological viewpoint, this combinatory play seems to be the essential feature in productive thought – before there is any connection with logical construction in words or other kinds of signs which can be communicated to others.

(B) The above-mentioned elements are, in my case, of visual and some of muscular type. Conventional words or other signs have to be sought for laboriously only in a secondary stage, when the mentioned associative play is sufficiently established and can be reproduced at will.

(C) According to what has been said, the play with the mentioned elements is aimed to be analogous to certain logical connections one is searching for.

(D) Visual and motor. In a stage when words intervene at all, they are, in my case, purely auditive, but they interfere only in a secondary stage, as already mentioned.

(E) It seems to me that what you call full consciousness is a limit case which can never be fully accomplished. This seems to me connected with the fact called the narrowness of consciousness (Enge des Bewusstseins).[20]

However, Einstein was also not able to provide a satisfactory answer on the selection mechanism in the unconscious, how does it see value, and what does this elevated insight and indeed wisdom consist of?

What more recent research proposes is that it appears that the unconscious somehow organises information in a better way than what conscious thought patterns do, it manages to polarise it into a more focus-based perspective through some filter mechanism of sort. This is through a form of automatic spreading activation along associative links where connecting chains are active to seek out unusual yet productive combinations. It also suggests that the unconscious holds the capability to process disorganised and incomplete information until it evolves into a better and better form of organisation which means some sort of equilibrium, or goal, might be reached that provides a signal to transfer the results thereof to the conscious part of the mind.[21,22] However, the aesthetic aspect of a creative solution as proposed by Poincaré comes with interesting and potentially valuable insights, as aesthetic qualities can be formulated operating towards certain laws that promote characteristics that align with harmonious symmetry.

COULD IT BE A PURELY CONSCIOUS EFFORT?

Whilst most, if not all, researchers of creativity agree that there is an incubation effect, documented through both anecdotal evidence and comprehensive studies, the crucial point remains on the degree of unconscious involvement to this effect.

The proponents of the incubation effect being a conscious-only endeavour point to that spending deliberate rational thinking on a problem and then wilfully neglecting it for a time helps to diminish a number of rational thought patterns and certain routines, that for the purpose of finding creative solutions offers relief from false content organising principles, and hence these augment the incubation effect.[23] The problem-solver might be cognitively drained and therefore unable to find a viable solution, so the stage of incubation is in essence a cognitive rest period which allows for rejuvenation that improves the likelihood for a creative solution.[24] However, what are then some of these constraining thought patterns that the proponents argue restrict creative possibilities?

- Abstractions to find uniformities across situations and thereby often ignore specific or unique aspects.
- Automatisation; relying on established patterns often of an almost reflex-like character, including knowledge and procedural skills that allow for effective actions to be taken in emergency situations.
- Bounded rationality; as humans only have limited cognitive resources, heuristics and rule of thumbs are routinely deployed to truncate reality, avoiding the complexities and intricacies of the real world.
- False assumptions are not unusually made during the preparation phase. These false assumptions erroneously constrain the possible solution space and prevent the problem-solver from producing correct solutions. Therefore, such erroneous assumptions must be allowed to be forgotten and hence relax restrictive thought patterns.
- Functional fixations; deploying the conventional interpretation of objects and situations and thus inhibiting the possibility for creative re-interpretations.
- Opportunistic assimilation; unsolved problems are often encoded in the long-term memory. As long as the problem remains, the resulting memory structure is primed and environmental clues that may be useful in solving the problem can easily activate the appropriate setting. Incubation is the period in which environmental clues are assimilated which enables the necessary details and hints to materialise that would otherwise have gone unnoticed without this priming.

- Remote association; solutions to already-solved problems are often stored in long-term memory. When a new problem is encountered, the previously stored solutions to similar problems are automatically retrieved. However, these solutions might be inappropriate and block the correct solution from being discovered. Less likely solutions are discovered only when the most likely solutions have all been investigated. The incubation phase is thus used to eliminate stereotypical erroneous solutions.

- Schemata are deployed as structures for representing stereotypical situations, reducing the understanding of the idiosyncrasy of the problem.[25,26]

So, a creative solution can be found when working intermittently on a problem while attending to mundane non-related activities, such as taking a stroll, going for a swim or to the gym, and so on. However, as attention switching from engaging in the trivial to the incubated problem is fast, the short micro-episodes of work on the problem tend to be forgotten, and only the final step, the actual solution is remembered, often appearing as a Eureka effect.

THE EXPLICIT–IMPLICIT INTERACTION THEORY

The Explicit–Implicit Interaction Theory (EII) was presented in 2010, in which the incubation phase is considered as involving unconscious, implicit, and stochastic associative processes that demand little attentional capacity, this in contrast to the conscious explicit rule governed attentionally demanding processes that run in parallel. The EII theory makes an attempt to integrate and thus unify other existing theories of creative problem-solving with their unconscious and conscious aspects into a holistic theory.[27]

THE BASIC PRINCIPLES OF EII

EII is organised around some formative principles, and the assumption is the existence of two different types of knowledge, explicit and implicit, residing in two separate vessels. Explicit knowledge is the easier to access and verbally articulate as being of a more abstract and definite nature. However, it requires an extensive use of attentional resources. Implicit knowledge is in contrast more difficult to access, not allowing for easy verbalisation, and lacking in precision, but it does not consume much attentional energy. Give their vastly different traits, explicit knowledge and implicit knowledge are processed differently. Explicit reasoning is generalised and rule-based, thus represented through an exact processing, often including hard constraints. The implicit processing is on the other hand associative and represents soft constraints satisfaction. With an understanding of the characteristics of explicit and implicit knowledge, the following principles can be outlined:

the coexistence of and the difference between explicit and implicit knowledge
1 the simultaneous involvement of implicit and explicit processes in most tasks;
2 the redundant representation of explicit and implicit knowledge;
3 the integration of the results of explicit and implicit processing; and
4 the iterative (and possibly bidirectional) processing.

To these there are three auxiliary principles:

5 The existence of a (rudimentary) metacognitive monitoring process;
6 The existence of subjective thresholds; and
7 The existence of a negative relation between confidence and response time.

Some of these principles require further comments:

• For principle 3), *the redundant representation of explicit and implicit knowledge.* In accordance with the EII theory, the redundancy is due to frequent re-descriptions between the different representational forms. For example, knowledge that is initially implicit is often later re-coded to form explicit knowledge, typically through bottom-up learning. Similarly, knowledge that is initially learned explicitly, such as through verbal instructions, is often later assimilated and established as an implicit form, usually after extensive practice, much as like learning how to ride a bicycle.

- For principle 4), the integration of the results of explicit and implicit processing. Although explicit knowledge and implicit knowledge are often re-descriptions of one another, they involve different forms of representation and processing, which may produce different conclusions.

- For principle 5), processing is often iterative and potentially bidirectional. If the integrated outcome of explicit and implicit processes does not yield a definitive result, such as a result in which one is highly confident, and if there is no time constraint, another round of processing may occur, which may often use the integrated outcome as a new input. Reversing the direction of reasoning may sometimes initiate this process, so-called abductive reasoning. Alternating between forward and backward processing has been argued to also happen in everyday reasoning.[28]

CREATIVITY AND MADNESS

The idea of the mad creative genius goes back to the ancient Greeks and perhaps even longer. The Greek philosopher Aristotle (384–322 BC) noted that many creative artists showed a streak of what was considered psychological disturbances of one sort or another, notably melancholy. He asked, probably rhetorically: how come all prominent men in philosophy, poetry, and art show signs of melancholy? This as what was considered being melancholic traits; reflective and introspective perspectives of thoughts were assumingly often found among the highly gifted. But then as now, the problem has been the blurred borders between madness, psychological ailments, eccentric behaviour, and the outer edges of normality, extending far and above the elusive labelling thereof. With the exception of the most obvious cases, which can be temporary bouts of deranged behaviour anyhow, there is a lack of crisp definitions of what is considered madness, and applying negative definitions such as deviations from normality does not provide much helpful guidance in understanding the nature of madness. However, the label "genius" can at least loosely be quantified as having an IQ level above 130. Madness, or today what is considered certain types of mental illnesses often in their milder forms, does through quite an extensive body of research point to a relationship with high IQ levels and associated creativity. This has led to the current view that certain types of mental illnesses, in particular links have been made between creativity and bipolar disorder and schizophrenia, hold the propensity to enhance creativity, but that they are not a prerequisite, a creative strand must already exist.[29,30,31]

That the subject still is considered intriguing can be noted from the broad and voluminous research that is being conducted, one Swedish study, including more than 1 million people, identified correlations between individuals performing typically creative work and mental ailments, as such, authors had a higher risk of anxiety, bipolar disorders, schizophrenia, unipolar depression, and substance abuse and were almost twice as likely as the general population to commit suicide. Dancers and photographers also had a higher likelihood to suffer from bipolar disorder. As a whole, however, members of creative professions were no more likely to experience psychiatric disorders than the general population, although they had a higher probability to have a close relative with a disorder of some negative mental impact, including anorexia and autism.[32]

Bipolar disorder, sometimes known as manic depression, is as mentioned above one of the mental ailments that has been linked to creative prowess, characterised by significant mood swings between euphoria where everything seems possible and depression when hopelessness colours perceptions, that phase can also include delusions, hallucinations, and paranoia. Mood-creativity research reveals, as expected, that people are most creative when they are in a positive mood and that depression decreases the levels of creative endeavours.[33,34]

Also, schizophrenia has been found to have links to creativity, which is characterised through hallucinations, delusions, thought, and movement disorders; in essence, one becomes detached from reality and withdrawn into oneself.[35,36] The schizophrenic often displays a sort of bizarre and strange behaviour, a kind of deviance from social norms and the standard way of living, which in benevolent terminology could be described as acting eccentric. They often come to display a certain abnormal awareness, in a sense a shared quality with the creating artist. However, whereas the artist chooses, controls, and uses certain states or forms of consciousness, the schizophrenic is having to suffer them, such as he appears to be controlled by his thoughts. Schizophrenics are also capable of a kind of extraordinary concentration, bringing with it a focus and awareness that is very difficult for non-sufferers to maintain, and they take pleasure in prolonged focus on specific objects.[37]

In *Madness and Modernism* (1992), the clinical psychologist Louis A. Sass noted that many common traits of schizophrenia, especially fragmentation, defiance of authority, and multiple viewpoints, also happen to be defining features of modern art.[38] Another study found creativity to be greater in schizotypal personalities than in either normal or schizophrenic individuals. Common for them is that they are obsessed with abstract, metaphysical, or technical concerns and are often bent on independence and originality, as such they remain completely indifferent to the opinions of others, avoiding conformity and herding behaviour. In schizotypy, it has been identified that the brain takes metaphorical leaps from domain to domain, making remote associations by using a broad attentional set. This is much in concurrence on how the unconscious is viewed to perform during the incubation phase in the search for creative solutions.[39,40]

Although some hints have been given how certain mental ailments can promote creative thinking, and enhance intellectual performance, there are more comprehensively documented psychological components in adverse mental conditions that stimulate creativity:

- *Compensatory adaptation*; as certain disabilities such as blindness or deafness can improve other senses, some mental ailments can elevate the ability to focus and access the unconscious.

- *Positive effects of mania*; mania if not too extreme comes with benefits as it produces quicker thinking, greater verbal fluency, and an ability to word play, an improved self-confidence, as well as optimism.
- *Knight's Move*; schizophrenia and bipolar disorder are characterised by sudden jumps in thought themes. These leaps from one idea to another can be quite unexpected, illogical, and are referred to as Knight's Move thinking. This way of thinking is important in the creative process because it enables a person to make connections without being anchored to preconceived ideas or being intellectually imprisoned by logical constraints.

The quality of creativity and achieving a level of genius seem to some extent to be about an ability to see beyond conventional thinking, disregarding cultural and scientific narratives, something which requires not only the perceptive trait of openness but also an intellectual capability of being able to do so. However, this openness to perspectives that contradict, even confront, customary conform thought practices has traditionally come with the risk of being regarded as mad, sometimes with dire consequences. Hence, the boundary between genius-level creativity and madness is indeed blurred.

The cognitive scientist Andrea Kuszewski noted in *The Essential Psychopathology of Creativity*:

> Were it not for those "disordered" genes, you wouldn't have extremely creative, successful people. Being in the absolute middle of every trait spectrum, not too extreme in any one direction, makes you balanced, but rather boring. The tails of the spectrum, or the fringe, is where all the exciting stuff happens. Some of the exciting stuff goes uncontrolled and ends up being a psychological disorder, but some of those people with the traits that define Bipolar Disorder, Schizophrenia, ADHD, and other psychological conditions, have the fortunate gift of high cognitive control paired with those traits, and end up being the creative geniuses that we admire, aspire to be like, and desperately need in this world.[41]

The phase of mania, or hypomania, as part of bipolarity provides an interesting case study as during mania, the levels of social inhibition decrease, making individuals both brazen and careless, allowing them to take risks, not unusually excessive, and confront social conventions. However, these symptoms are not equivalent to a fully developed psychopathology which comes with significant impairments that would hinder creative ventures.[42,43] As the speed of thinking accelerates, it allows for word association to form more freely, as well as flight of ideas, as a mind operating on a mania overdrive is less focused on filtering out thoughts and details that would otherwise be deemed irrelevant from the conscious mind's rational perspective of preconceived notions.[44] A study from 2017 demonstrated that mild to moderate mental illnesses increase the production of divergent thoughts. The researcher highlighted that:

> ... the "wavering attention and day-dreamy state" of ADHD, for example, "is also a source of highly original thinking. Their creativity, out-of-the-box thinking, high energy levels, and disinhibited manner could all be a positive result of their negative affliction."[45]

The flows of thoughts are usually marked through loose associations, and the individual with mania keeps changing subjects; however, they somehow relate, albeit often in a farfetched manner, making it hard for others to follow. Typical is also that many in a manic state become notedly energetic, with little need for sleep. At the early phase of mania, the performance at work usually improves notably, fuelled by a temporary excessive drive for winning and success, something which lasts until the mania takes a full grip of the personality.[46] The manic phase is eventually followed by a depressive and gloomy state of mood, which completely reverses the energetic bursts into lethargy and dullness. Anecdotally, patterns of mania have been noted features for many (successful) entrepreneurs; however, it is usually in its milder forms, colloquially being deemed as crazy enough to start a startup, a statistically well-recognised high-risk undertaking.[47] The (hypo)manic condition is often described as unleashing creative capacity and performance.[48] It somehow allows for thinking outside the box, emotions get stronger, and there is often not only a quantitative but also a qualitative improvement in ideas, producing uniqueness and value-adding. The capacity for combinatorial thinking is elevated, with odd perceptions and ideas being brought together and allowing them to find potential for symbiosis.[49,50] The acknowledged characteristics of creative cognition share the manic phase's racing thoughts more than schizophrenia's looser associations. Mania in itself does not produce creativity, for a person that normally displays no propensity for creative endeavours, the manic phase will for him not release creative ideas; however, for an already creative person, the mania can help produce some of his most highly innovative work. In fact, truly intense phases of creativity can be almost impossible to distinguish from hypomania, highlighted through the flow of ideas, the focus, the energy, the emotions, and the restlessness, all manifested through the enablement of the audacious and daring personality willing to take on the associated risks.[51,52]

CONCLUSIONS

Creativity includes an element of transgression which means previous thought patterns and preconceived notions are challenged and eventually disregarded, and a new thought paradigm comes to rule our narrative. The jury is out on how the creative spark ignites, but it appears to carry some unconscious tenets, as even the conscious-only proponents are at a loss to fully model the identification of suitable solutions. Instead associative-based thinking that somehow is actively searching for "aesthetic" solutions appears to be at work and happening beyond our active control. The capacity for being able to generate highly abstract creative solutions requires not only domain expertise but also sufficient cognitive levels, and it explains why despite governmental efforts around the world to promote creativity, so few engage in successful innovative and entrepreneurial work.

The mystery thus remains, but the next chapter will explore how creativity appears in very different settings, and this gives a useful perspective, albeit in a plethora of different jargon, on the mechanics that trigger it which will form the blueprint to establish computational creativity.

NOTES

1 Kuhn, Thomas S. *The Structure of Scientific Revolutions* (Chicago: University of Chicago Press, 1962).

2 Maslow, Arthur. *Toward a Psychology of Being* (New York: Wiley, 1962).

3 Adler, Alfred. *The Individual Psychology of Alfred Adler* (New York: Harper Torchbooks, 1964).

4 Öllinger, Michael, Volz, Kirsten, & Szathmáry, Eörs. Insight and Intuition – Two Sides of the Same Coin? (*Frontiers in Psychology*, 9, 2018), p. 689.

5 Ibid.

6 Topolinski, Sascha & Strack, Fritz. The Analysis of Intuition: Processing Fluency and Affect in Judgments of Semantic Coherence (*Cognition and Emotion*, 23(8), December 2009), pp. 1465–1503.

7 Gigerenzer, G. Why Heuristics Work (*Perspectives on Psychological Science*, 3(1), January 1, 2008), pp. 20–29.

8 Claxton, G. L. Investigating Human Intuition: Knowing without Knowing Why (*Psychologist*, 11(5), 1998), pp. 217–220.

9 Gigerenzer, G. & Selten, R. (Eds). *Bounded Rationality: The Adaptive Toolbox* (Cambridge: MIT Press, 2001).

10 Kruglanski A. W. & Gigerenzer, G. Intuitive and Deliberate Judgments Are Based on Common Principles (*Psychological Review*, 118(1), January 2011), pp. 97–109.

11 Öllinger, Michael & von Müller, Albrecht. Search and Coherence-Building in Intuition and Insight Problem Solving (*Frontiers in Psychology*, 8, 2017), p. 827.

12 Jung-Beeman, M., et al. Neural activity when people solve verbal problems with insight (*Biology*, 2, 2004), pp. 500–510.

13 Öllinger, Michael, Volz, Kirsten & Szathmáry, Eörs. Insight and Intuition – Two Sides of the Same Coin? (*Frontiers in Psychology*, 9, 2018), p. 689.

14 Dijksterhuis, A. & Nordgren, L.F. A Theory of Unconscious Thought Perspectives (*Psychological Science*, 1(2), June 2006), pp. 95–109.

15 Ritter, S.M., van Baaren, R. B., & Dijksterhuis, A. Creativity: The Role of Unconscious Processes in Idea Generation and Idea Selection (*Think. Skills Creativity*, 7, 2012), pp. 21–27.

16 Segal, E. Incubation in Insight Problem Solving (*Creativity Research Journal*, 16(1), 2004), pp. 141–148.

17 Ritter, S. M. & Dijksterhuis, A. Creativity-The Unconscious Foundations of the Incubation Period (*Frontiers in Human Neuroscience*, 8, 2014), p. 215.

18 Poincaré, Henri. Mathematical Creation (*The Monist*, 20, 1910), pp. 321–335.

19 Wertheimer, Max. *Productive Thinking* (New York: Harper, 1945).

20 Hadamard, Jacques. The Psychology of Invention in the Mathematical Field (*Philosophy and Phenomenological Research*, 10(2), 1949), pp. 288–289.

21 Gilhooly, Kenneth J. Incubation and Intuition in Creative Problem Solving (*Frontiers in Psychology*, 7, 2016), p. 1076.

22 Sio, U.N. & Ormerod, T.C. Does Incubation Enhance Problem Solving? A Meta-Analytic Review (*Psychological Bulletin*, 135(1), January 2009), pp. 94–120.

23 Segal, E. Incubation in Insight Problem Solving (*Creativity Research Journal*, 16(1), 2004), pp. 141–148.

24 Hélie, S. & Sun, R. Incubation, Insight, and Creative Problem Solving: A Unified Theory and a Connectionist Model (*Psychological Review*, 117(3), 2010), pp. 994–1024.

25 Smith, S. M. & Dodds, R. A. Incubation (In M. A. Runco & S. R. Pritzker (Eds.), *Encyclopedia of Creativity*, San Diego, CA: Academic Press, 1999), pp. 39–43.

26 Langley, P. Systematic and Nonsystematic Search Strategies (In J. Hendler (Ed.), *Intelligence Planning Systems: Proceedings of the First International Conference*, Burlington, MA: Morgan Kaufmann Pub, 1992), pp. 145–152.

27 Hélie, S. & Sun, R. Incubation, Insight, and Creative Problem Solving: A Unified Theory and a Connectionist Model (*Psychological Review*, 117(3), 2010), pp. 994–1024.

28 Ibid.

29 Neus, Barrantes Vidal. Creativity & Madness Revisited from Current Psychological Perspectives (*Journal of Consciousness Studies*, 11(3–4), January 2004), pp. 58–78.

30 Claridge, G. & Blakey, S. Schizotypy and Affective Temperament: Relationships with Divergent Thinking and Creativity Styles (*Personality and Individual Differences*, 46(8), 2009), pp. 820–826.

31 Nelson, B. & Rawlings, D. Relating Schizotypy and Personality to the Phenomenology of Creativity (Schizophrenia Research, 36, 2010), pp. 388–399.

32 Kyaga, S., Lichtenstein, P., Boman, M., Hultman, C., Långström, N., & Landén, M. Creativity and Mental Disorder: Family Study of 300 000 People with Severe Mental Disorder (The British Journal of Psychiatry, 199(5), 2011), pp. 373–379.

33 Davis, Mark A. Understanding the Relationship between Mood and Creativity: A Meta-Analysis (Organizational Behavior and Human Decision Processes, 100(1), January 2009), pp. 25–38.

34 Baas, Matthijs, De Dreu Carsten, K. W., & Nijstad, Bernard A. A Meta-Analysis of 25 Years of Mood-Creativity Research: Hedonic Tone, Activation, or Regulatory Focus? (Psychological Bulletin, 134 (6), November 2008), pp. 779–806.

35 Furnham, Batey M. The Relationship between Creativity, Schizotypy and Intelligence (Individual Differences Research, 7, 2009), pp. 272–284.

36 Furnham, Batey M., Anand, K., & Manfield, J. Personality, Hypomania, Intelligence and Creativity (Personality and Individual Differences, 44(5), 2008), pp. 1060–1069.

37 Sass, Louis A. Madness and Modernism: Insanity in the Light of Modern Art, Literature, and Thought (New York: Basic Books, 1st edition, 1992).

38 Parker, G. (Ed.). Bipolar II Disorder: Modeling, Measuring and Managing (Cambridge: Cambridge University Press, 2005).

39 Runco, M. A. Creativity and Reason in Cognitive Development (Cambridge: Cambridge University Press, 2006), pp. 99–116.

40 Nettle, Daniel. An Evolutionary Approach to the Extraversion Continuum (Evolution and Human Behavior, 26(4), July 2005), pp. 363–373.

41 Kuszewski, Andrea. The Essential Psychopathology of Creativity, 2010. https://ieet.org/index.php/IEET2/more/kuszewski20100928 (accessed 1 April 2021).

42 Mental Health Information. Schizophrenia. https://www.nimh.nih.gov/health/topics/schizophrenia/index.shtml#part_145430 (accessed 1 April 2021)

43 Frey, Angelica. A New Account of Robert Lowell's Mania Risks Glorifying It (Hyperallergic, May 3, 2017).

44 Parker, G. (Ed.) Bipolar II Disorder: Modeling, Measuring and Managing (Cambridge: Cambridge University Press, 2005).

45 Jamison, Kay Redfield. Touched with Fire: Manic-Depressive Illness and the Artistic Temperament (New York: Free Press, 1996).

46 American Psychiatric Association. *DSM-5 Update: Supplement to Diagnostic and Statistical Manual of Mental Disorders* (Philadelphia, PA: American Psychiatric Association Publishing, 5th edition, 2016).

47 Segal, David. *Just Manic Enough: Seeking Perfect Entrepreneurs* (New York Times, 18 September 2018).

48 Goodwin, Frederick K. & Redfield Jamison, Kay. *Manic-Depressive Illness - Bipolar Disorders and Recurrent Depression* (New York: Oxford University Press, 95, 2007), pp. 90–98.

49 Fazel, Seena, Goodwin, Guy M., Grann, Martin, Lichtenstein, Paul, & Långström, Niklas. Bipolar Disorder and Violent Crime: New Evidence from Population-Based Longitudinal Studies and Systematic Review (*Archives of General Psychiatry*, 67, September 7, 2010), pp. 931–938.

50 Mathers, Colin D., Ezzati, Majid, Jamison, Dean T., & Myrray, Christopher J. L. *Global Burden of Disease and Risk Factors* (New York: Oxford University Press and The World Bank, 2006), p. 70.

51 de Manzano, Ö., Cervenka, S., Karabanov, A., Farde, L., & Ullén, F. *Samband mellan psykisk ohälsa och kreativitet*, 2010. https://ki.se/nyheter/samband-mellan-psykisk-ohalsa-och-kreativitet (accessed 1 April 2021)

52 Goodwin, Frederick K. & Redfield Jamison, Kay. *Manic-Depressive Illness - Bipolar Disorders and Recurrent Depression* (New York: Oxford University Press, 95, 2007), pp. 90–98.

3

PERSPECTIVES ON CREATIVITY

Creativity is just connecting things.
    Steve Jobs, iconic visionary and digital leader (1955–2011)

Creativity does of course manifest in many different varieties, and each of these has developed its own interpretation of the creative process and ways to embrace it. This covers not only science but also the many facets of arts extending into literature and linguistics and even religious experiences.

CREATIVE ART

The original function of art was magic, and some of the remaining traces of the first examples of art that have been discovered are depictions of animals that our stone-age ancestors hoped to track down and kill for food. This was magical thinking about future events they hoped for and imagined to materialise, something which later on extended to organised religion, and for a long time, religious themes were the main focus of art. Purely secular art is a relatively new phenomenon that has only been in existence for about the last three centuries. Art was, and is, produced with the aim to be eternal, aspiring

DOI: 10.1201/9781003194941-4

outside the realms of what we can fathom, and towards appeasing the divine ethereal. It was considered that to produce such art, it actually required divine powers which only were bestowed to certain humans through inspiration that comes upon them spontaneously. In that perspective, humans were not the true creators but only acted as vessels for the divine. Later on, the Swiss psychologist Carl Gustav Jung argued that what was seen as divine unexplainable forces was actually drawn from the unconscious part of the human mind, and so he described the condition of creation;

> No genius has ever sat down with a pen or a brush in his hand and said: "Now I a m going to invent a symbol." No one can take a more or less rational thought, reached as a logical conclusion or by deliberate intent, and then give it "symbolic" form. No matter what fantastic trappings one may put upon an idea of this kind, it will still remain a sign, linked to the conscious thought behind it, not a symbol that hints at something not yet known.[1]

In a study of artists and their works by the Swedish psychologist Gudmund Smith (1920–2012), he noticed that their motifs often appear to connect to earlier experiences in life that in some ways have deviated from the concept of normality. Smith argued that these experiences allowed them the child-like unprejudiced view of reality by combining seemingly incompatible perspectives to break deadlocks and open new angles to consider the world around them. The Swedish artist Violet Tengberg (1920–2014) expressed it as she was a vehicle for something unspoken that however still was present and she sought to depict. During the act of creation, the artist enters a stage much like being in the proverbial zone, where the focus on oneself dims out and full attention is turned to the creative work. Hence, the artistic creative process, sometimes both immediate and spontaneous, is the conduit which enables the artist to acknowledge and craft this unspoken phenomenon. However, it might not be obvious during the process itself, as it is first when the artwork is completed and been contemplated that it becomes comprehensible for the rational mind, also sometimes for the artists themselves.[2] The Russian artist Wassily Kandinsky (1866–1944) wrote in his famous paper *Concerning the spiritual in art* (Über das Geistige in der Kunst) from 1911 that he regarded art as a tool for spiritual renewal in society, this at a time when Christianity in Europe was in noted decline:

> The artist can as part of his genius create what breaks existing rules and give rise to new norms. The difference between the genial and the bizarre is exposed through the meaning that the piece of art can promote, an experience which might change over time.[3]

Kandinsky referred to a spiritual reality at risk of fading from the collective mind and argued that objects hold spiritual characteristics. However, his explanations of the spiritual in art remained obscure and vague as he was deploying emotional and poetic language to describe its effects. The key to art for him was spontaneity, and he put a lot of emphasis on using one's intuition in the creation of art. Kandinsky argued that the soul comprehends the spiritual qualities in art and objects, much as sight and hearing appreciate favourable audible and viewable perceptions, and also the soul had these sensatory qualities. Hence, the artist can never create something new, he will merely convey and display elements of the spiritual world, and therefore he is serving a higher cause, however, with differing themes depending on time epoque and culture. Therefore, the artist's work process was to turn inwards and directing his attention towards the soul, trying to identify the notions and reflexes from the spiritual world which could embrace anyone, and it was his task to craft these insights in colours, forms, and thematic patterns. The true reward to an artist, beyond fame and commercial success, was being equipped with an elevated soul, purified and ennobled through the struggle, and painstakingly demanding efforts to reach the spiritual world and then depict it in a titillating manner. It would also refine the artist's emotional spectra, such that broad-brushed feelings such as anxiety, happiness, and sorrow would be diminishing, and it would enable him to rise above these, aspiring to form more subtle emotions and mindsets that were so complex that they were yet to be defined and adequately labelled. By reflecting on this spiritual world through the efforts of painting, it provided Kandinsky with a path to the abstract. His contemporary, the Russian painter Kazimir Malevich (1879–1935) shared his goals that through art, a hidden spiritual world that is being obscured behind everyday objects can be unmasked, expressing a bridge between micro cosmos and macro cosmos, "as above – as below", a vision which generally has been shared by other mystics throughout time. Differing from Kandinsky's passion of abstract art with its colours and dissolving forms, Malevich focused on geometric forms, both in its scientific display and through alchemic mathematical interpretations, leading to an art perspective which he endorsed as suprematism. Its building blocks consisted of quadrants, circles, and the cross, and by distorting these in various formations, Malevich created an artistic style of radical geometric abstracts, both materialistic and spiritual, labelled 'suprematistic forms'. To him these represented the feelings' objects, and suprematism whilst admittedly intranslatable came to broadly mean "the pure supremacy". To Malevich, it was the role of man to understand the laws and forces of universe, and the quest of an artist to endorse and reflect them. As such, through suprematism, he aspired to reveal that the world is really void of objects. Given his Russian background, his art could be regarded as icons; and whilst religious orthodox aspects were missing, they gave notions of dimensions of time and space beyond our immediate world. Expanding on the geometric forms as art, later on both artists and mathematicians were seeking aesthetic values in mathematics, where symmetry and complexity are prized characteristics, extending to the concept of mathematical beauty, where this concept was equaled with mathematical truth. From a mathematical point of view, it at times came down to that both beauty and truth are influenced by processing eloquence, which measures the ease with which information can be processed. And some mathematical patterns, such as The Fibonacci Patterns or The Mandelbrot Fractals, show symmetric forms which represent what is considered treasured aesthetic qualities, and this has for some academics served as an evidence that beauty indeed can highlight truths in mathematics.[4,5,6]

Among art critiques, it is often this unspoken element that when eloquently displayed provides an artwork its merits. Deliberate attempts to producing this type of art seeking to purposely display the obscure by taking it to the forefront with the view of creating a speculative stir rarely stand the test of time and in hindsight will often be ridiculed. This, as it is the true unexplainable residue that intrigues the art lover and which makes art so interesting, even mesmerising, as it somehow resonates with the unconscious, but that rational language itself only rarely can properly convey. The unspoken often reflects covert elements in the reigning time epoch and is often accompanied by prophetic visions of the future bringing an eerie excitement that tends to excite the audience. How it is artistically manifested whether as paintings, music, or poetry will depend on the level of freedom, marked in the manner the artist is allowed to express himself, and sometimes expanding beyond, and indeed his technical skill. Surrealism was another art form that deployed the unspoken features in that it combined two worlds that led to enticing interpretations as it triggered a kaleidoscopic perspective. In the surrealistic creative process, isolation of objects from their natural setting is the first step by deploying a great variation of rules and routines. It is displayed as a collage arrangement, and the surrealists often used images from photos that have been segregated from their narratives. The object in question was considered "liberated" and could then be observed from unusual perspectives. In that sense, they were psychological displacements, which are redirections where an object shifts aim and meaning.[7]

In the German-Israeli psychologist Erich Neumann's (1905–1960) work *Art and The Creative Unconscious*, he deployed many Freudian and Jungian concepts in arguing for the unconscious influence on the creation of art. He, through providing a number of historical examples, claimed that the hypothesis of the creative function of the unconscious was utilised in these works, as it is capable of producing art spontaneously once accessed. Neumann's theory has its roots in the Jungian concept of a collective unconscious, acclaimed of being the source of mental energy, manifesting itself through symbols and leaving it to humans able to access it to express it in various fashions including religion, social establishments, and the arts. The collective conscious on the other side provided the cultural canon, the contexts, and narrative in which the symbols could be embedded providing transformations and even revolutions to counter a stagnating culture. Neumann expressed it as:

> When unconscious forces breakthrough in the artist, when the archetypes striving to be born into the light of the world take form in him, he is as far from the men around him as he is close to their destiny. For he expresses and gives form to the future of his epoch.[8]

The creative individual becomes an instrument of this shared collective unconscious force that grabs hold of him through provoking impulses that capture humans at the subliminal level and create an emotionally stir with its contemporaries. The psychological factor for creative work is therefore pivotal. When the artist manages to embrace these unconscious signals and artistically represent them, his artwork holds the propensity of reaching the level of timelessness. The irruption of material of the unconscious to the conscious is marked by a suddenness and indeed strangeness, this irruption represents only the "bursting point" of a transformative process that has long been present but has not previously been perceptible at the level of awareness. Every transformative or creative process comprises of certain levels of possession. To be captivated and spellbound signifies what it is to be possessed by something, and without such a fascination and the emotional tension connected with it, the exceptional ability for extended focus which more often than not serves as the edifice for the creative process and its successful outcome is deemed unlikely. Every possession can justifiably be interpreted either as a one-sided narrowing or as an intensification and deepening of thought towards a creative solution.[9]

The Austrian-British philosopher Karl Popper (1902–1994) studied creativity and noted the resemblance between the creative process in art and in science with its trial-and-error process in finding
solutions; *The difference between the amoeba and Einstein is that although both
make use of the method of trial-and-error elimination, the amoeba dislikes to err while
Einstein is intrigued by it: he consciously searches for his errors in the hope of learning
by discovery and elimination.*[10]

He acknowledged the importance of the trial-and-error process,
but the identification of a solution, and often not finding a solution
at all, remained enigmatic. He referred to an intellectual intuition that
needed to be in place, the sorting mechanism of a myriad of potential
options. Popper argued that creative individuals appeared to have that
cognisant ability to make distinguished selection far ahead that of their
lesser creative peers. It appeared to be above and beyond rational inference and reasoning, as it is transcending a sequential decision-making
process. In short, it was about finding a structure to arrange the reigning chaos around. Popper also added an interesting moral and psychological aspect on creativity, highlighting that an innovative capability
goes beyond ingenious insights and brilliant ideas, as these might
come many individuals but the majority often lack the courage to act
on them, and hence never allow them to properly manifest. Thus, what
additionally is required is a will and courage to true self-expression.

RELIGIOUS MYSTICISM

However, the tenets of the creative process can also be noted in religion, notably revelations and similar experiences labelled as mysticism. Mysticism is an ambiguous term, but it is a feature found
in all known religions, with its typically shaman-like practitioners
claiming access to divine forces and often being trusted to interpret
their intentions. The word mysticism has Greek roots meaning to
conceal, highlighting that the experience somehow triggers a (sudden) revelation or insight that provides an elevated knowledge of an
extraordinary nature. Mysticism is seen to align spiritual practices
with an inner meaning, the absolute truths of the particular religious

doctrine, but there is not yet a definition of it that has been commonly agreed upon among academia and religious practitioners. The religious mystical manifestations are usually culturally distinct, but they aim to bring with them a higher insight, an improved spiritual understanding, and in that sense, they share similarities with artistic and scientific breakthroughs, being an elevation of knowledge. It is generally agreed that religious mystical experiences are not accessible through normal rational thought patterns, but it is something that is prompted through other means of deliberation. A highly esoteric take of mysticism is to regard it as a union with God, or the Absolute, which can only occur under a state of altered consciousness. And here lies the goal of mysticism, the *unio mystica*, the unmediated unity with God, which implicitly assumes that humans exist in a world where there by default is a gap between the divine and mankind which can only be accessed through special means.[11,12,13]

The unio mystica functions as an uncoupling of the divine element within man and is released through gaining insight. Mystics emphasise that their quest for unio mystica must be conducted with great dedication but at the same time they must abstain from expectations, indeed a delicate balance. Therefore, to intellectually try to think a mystic experience into fruition is seen as an obstacle towards enlightenment.[14] The mystical experience allows for an expanding inward-looking awareness at the expense of a diminishing perception of the external world, almost to the point of shutting it down. The sensations are often accompanied by a euphoric mood. Religious scholars have noted that our language rarely suffices to explain mystical experiences, and mystics therefore must resort to metaphors and other symbolic language to describe their visions and similar. This vague and pictorial language thus indirectly highlights the characteristic of the mystic experience, its indescribability. That our language lacks the capacity to accurately describe it likely means that it is beyond our comprehension to convey as there is a certain irrational aspect that is somehow out of scope for our rational thought system to fully explain. God, or the divine, is therefore often described in negations, by what it is not.[15] The deployment of metaphors to describe mystical experiences can in themselves destabilise us by undermining our preconceptions, which then contradictorily enough increases the possibility to connect to the essence of the divine forces.[16] The American biblical scholar Jouette Bassler wrote in her *The Parable of the Loaves* that:

> …a metaphor communicates by juxtaposing two not entirely comparable elements, thereby inducing the hearer to extract from the somewhat discordant image a new vision of the primary element.[17]

Hence, the symbolic language harbours the root of mysticism in carrying a tension between what is known and what is not, and this conundrum between opposites can attract an engagement.

The German-American theologian Paul Tillich (1886–1965) wrote eloquently about religious symbolism highlighting key elements to understand their meaning and significance:

- they point to something beyond themselves;
- they participate in that to which they point;
- symbols open up levels of reality that otherwise are closed to us; and
- they also open up the levels and dimensions of the soul that correspond to those levels of reality.[18]

This requires that symbols are active, when they no longer can produce a response as suggested above, they must be considered dead symbols that no longer can resonate with us.[19] Thus, symbolic language and indeed other manifests of symbolism are necessary as they function as catalysts, and without them it becomes difficult to connect to these spiritual dimensions and mystical experiences. Tillich saw them as following a set path:

- point;
- participate;

- open up;
- unlock;
- produce;
- grow; and then finally
- die.[20]

This unpredictability of symbols, in essence chaos, eventually seeks to bring with it an order and structure. Therefore, symbols first generate chaos, and then attempt to build symmetry by acting as interfaces through mediating between the conscious and unconscious parts of the mind. The German literary scholar Wolfgang Iser (1926–2007) theorised that when there are gaps in a story, an implicit dialogue between the text and the readers occurs, they are having to relate to the clear distinction between the written and unwritten part of the text. When the reader's expectation of the text is not fulfilled and discontinuities appear, the reader starts to fill in what appears to be missing in the text vis-à-vis his expectations, and the text takes a sort of life of its own. In that sense, the reader goes from passive to active, and with religious symbolism it works much the same, leaving us to fill in the void, hence why the interpretation tends to differ between individuals, and this filling in of the void becomes an integral part of the mystic experience. Hence, the chaos generated between reader and text leads to the discovery of new symmetries (read: meaning) between them. Chaos is therefore the dynamics required to create meaning. Symbols will through their ambiguities seek to bridge this divide by finding arrays of meaning in chaos.[21,22]

The feeling of being drawn towards something that resists definition can often provide the sensation of being the object of an intention other than one's own, an agency that can generate an attraction to something above and beyond oneself. To Freud, this was the phenomena of the uncanny that provided the ambiguity of simultaneously feeling both anxiety and attraction, something that provided familiarity and a strangeness at the same time. The unconscious part of a symbol is therefore seen as holding a covert (religious) meaning, but the interpretation will differ between individuals, where the more perceptive will acknowledge it and others not. Here we need to draw the distinction between the conscious and unconscious perspectives, as according to CG Jung, the conscious analyses phenomena with the objective of breaking it down to its component parts and providing it with definitions, hence it acts as a differentiator making distinctions. The unconscious however integrates and synthesises components into new combinations with a synergetic effect, in essence, they exceed the sum of the individual components. However, the value and design of the synergetic combinations are not necessarily forecastable from the components themselves and will only be verifiable in a hindsight rational conscious analysis. Symbols interconnecting these two perspectives can then function as a psychological mechanism that transforms psychological energy. It therefore requires us to be able to confront the unknown and accept operating in a chaotic environment where the outcomes cannot be exactly forecasted.[23] However, there is no conclusive contradiction between mysticism and rational thought, the Greek philosopher Plato argued that discursive thought is a prerequisite to reach the insight of mysticism and that it will in reverse complete and form the basis for rational thought.[24]

The German theologian Rudolf Otto (1869–1937) published in 1917 what has remained one of the leading works of religious mysticism *The Idea of the Holy* (Das Heilige – Über das Irrationale in der Idee des Göttlichen und sein Verhältnis zum Rationalen), and he coined the term "numinous" which he explains as a "non-rational, non-sensory experience or feeling whose primary and immediate object is outside the self", in effect being the innermost core of religion. The numinous experience has two aspects:

- *mysterium tremendum*, which is the tendency to invoke fear and trembling; and
- *mysterium fascinans*, the tendency to attract, fascinate, and compel.[25]

Another work which still remains authoritative is the American psychologist cum philosopher William James' (1842–1910), *The Varieties of Religious Experience* from 1902, which is a collection of lectures, in it he classified the characteristics of a mystical experience as:

- transient; the experience is temporary; the individual soon returns to a "normal" frame of mind. The experience feels outside normal perception of space and time;
- ineffable; the experience cannot be adequately put into words;
- noetic; the individual feels that he has learned something valuable from the experience by gaining a knowledge that is normally hidden from human understanding; and
- passive; the experience happens largely without conscious control. Although there are activities, such as meditation that can facilitate mysticism, the experience cannot be deliberately provoked into action.[26]

A key requisite for reaching a mystic experience is the achievement of a changing mode of consciousness. The American psychiatrist Arthur J. Deikman (1929–2013) highlighted five features of the mystical experience:

1 intense realness;
2 unusual sensations;
3 unity;
4 ineffability; and
5 trans-sensate phenomena.[27]

These features were much in concurrence with James' characteristics of a mystic experience. The intense feeling of realness and unusual sensations during a mystic experience often include perceptions of encompassing lights and infinite energy that accompanies the visions. In all, an encounter that differs starkly from any other phenomena that can be experienced in everyday life.

That the thought patterns involved in a mystical experience appear different than discursive thinking, is an observation shared by most academics. The American philosopher of religion, Robert M. Gimello stated that the mystic experience is characterised, among other things, by "a cessation of normal intellectual operation" such as deduction, discrimination, and speculation, with the substitution of them to some qualitatively different mode of intellect, such as intuition and sudden revelations. This mystic thinking mode also brings with it an improvement of attention and focus, a type of 'being in the zone' effect.[28]

The mystic experience relates to "the death of the Ego" and is often followed by a spiritual rebirth. The Italian psychiatrist Silvano Arieti (1914–1981) divided the human cognitive processes into three main categories: the primary process that dominates certain states of mental illnesses and is the foundation for dreams. The secondary process is represented by normal consciousness adjusting to the perceptions of reality. Both these processes are aligned with the Freudian aspects of an unconscious and conscious part of the human mind, and then Arieti introduced the tertiary process, responsible for the "magic synthesis" of primary and secondary processes being the springboard of creativity. In Arieti's own words, the creative process is structured as follows:

> Instead of rejecting the primitive (or whatever is archaic, obsolete, or off the beaten path), the creative mind integrates it with normal logical processes in what seems a 'magic' synthesis from which the new, the unexpected, and the desirable emerge.[29]

To apply the creative perspectives on these experiences of mysticism, seeking a common framework to understand the nature of creativity, Wallas' theory has been applied on religious experiences by the American social psychologist C. Daniel Batson and the American psychology professor W. Larry Ventis. They suggested that the four stages of Wallas' creative process can be compared with a religious conversion. A human searching for religious truths concurs with the scientist's search for scientific truths and insights, the process is essentially the same, just that the former is typically dealing with existential problems and their solutions. In the illuminative phase, the religious visions appear, after a number of failed trails to search and find religious meaning which lead to despair and a sense of hopelessness, and eventually bring about an unobtrusive humility. This surrender of the *Ego* facilitates the prospects of insight and the start of a religious life aligning with the preferred religious doctrine. This new perspective allows for the return back to everyday life, but the newly converted is now equipped with an increased degree of certainty of a religious afterlife, which typically tends to embrace a more harmonic lifestyle. Batson and Ventis highlighted that the feeling of anxiety and the dramatic turn to ecstatic joy and passion are pivotal moments in the religious experience. The relationship between cognition and emotion is accentuated through these strong feelings that motivate the individual to make changes to one's life, the transformation. The visions therefore create order in a psychological environment of chaos.[30]

AUTOMATISATION AND DE-AUTOMATISATION

Through the mystic experience, its practitioners claim that their perceptions of reality are altered, allowing for the perceived enlightenment to materialise. From various studies and traditions, it appears that they shift focus through the altered selection of perceptions and stimuli, which typically is governed and constrained through normative and social habits and rules. Given the brain's memory limitations, we are forced to focus our attention span on certain phenomena and reject others, this selection mechanism is often culturally induced, meaning that representatives from different cultures would not only make different selections of perceptions, but also have differing interpretations and meanings of identical perceptions. This process becomes automated, which makes it hard for us to override it and manipulate it at will. Thus, automatisation is formed through stereotypical interpretations of reality, and as mentioned often imposed through cultural constraints, and is utilised to facilitate the understanding and interpretation of stimuli, seeking out shared features rather than their uniqueness. It takes dedicated efforts to break this automatisation process, as it exists to conserve energy in order to optimise efficiency. It has been argued that the mystical process seeks to de-automise these thought patterns, as it then would allow for a differing perspective of reality to occur which for the religiously inclined would be conditioned on spiritual matters. Therefore, it engages in perception selection and cognitive patterns, because a force with such strong underlying motivation requires special efforts to circumvent a reflex-like process. De-automatisation aims to break down or ignore these automated patterns but given that they have a biological grounding, the exemptions can thus only exist temporarily. It can be considered that as part of the intense spiritual focus as well as practice through meditation exercises, the capacity for a receptive mode function would increase, leading to a heightened attention span and absorption of details.[31,32]

The de-automation brings with it a level of chaos through the undoing of existing arrangements towards something unknown. However, by breaking up the fragmentating structures, an aspiration towards unity is achieved which is mysticism's objective. This move from individual component levels to finding common ground between the objects, whether abstract or not, seeks to dissolve all boundaries until any constraints of the conscious part of the mind no longer are viewed as a separate entity with the comme-il-faut perceptual and cognitive distinctions abating.[33]

The American psychiatrist Louis Jolyon West (1924–1999) launched a theory that sensory input can be impaired through overloading the mind or by under-stimulating it. This could manifest as persisting repetitive prayers, often combined with specific body movements, ecstatic dance, or breathing techniques, allowing for automatisation to be relaxed, through causing an input overload. This overstimulation can also be reflected in creative work as individuals engage in an intensive struggle with a problem in an active perceptive mode, and when one has consciously arrived at a dead end, self-surrender occurs and a receptive mode ensues with the possibility that the productive answer can suddenly arise, establishing the creative synthesis, representing Wallas incubation phase. But also, the contrast to overstimulation, under-stimulation can bring about de-automatisation, highlighted through examples where solitary confinement can produce hallucinatory phantasies and visions.[34]

LITERATURE AND LINGUISTICS

Magic language is an interesting concept as it is so distinct from scientific language in that it is emotional and converts words into symbols, and it is therefore particularly apt at constructing metaphors and other figurative language. The symbols often represent challenging, even disturbing phases, typically touching and provoking existing taboos. It is thus suitable to describe the unspoken, the unknown knowns, and it is often considered being a seemingly weird language. The Polish anthropologist Bronisław Malinowski (1884–1942) described the magic language as possessing a high "coefficient of weirdness" meaning it is archaic in nature and out of the ordinary. This weirdness is seen as necessary to effect changes in the human mind by appealing to forces in the unconscious. Thus, the magic vocabulary always appears antagonistic to the reigning narrative and can be perceived as sinister and its practitioners seen as atavistic by its contemporary. The true magic is therefore always implausible, a "black swan" event of sorts, but through conjuring repressed unconscious themes to surface into awareness, it can tilt previous unthought scenarios into existence.[35]

Magical language, according to the English linguist Charles Kay Ogden (1889–1957) and the English literary critic Ivor. A. Richards (1893–1979), being of such ambiguous nature will play an important transcending role in transmitting meaning to what previously has lacked description and definition, typically by applying metaphors. It is constructed by principles such as the Law of Similarity, in which the magician infers that he can produce any effect he desires merely by imitating it, and the Law of Contact or Contagion, where the magician infers that whatever he does to an object will affect equally the person with whom the object was once in contact.[36] Magic rests on the belief that reality can be influenced if one finds a way that it forms a comprehensible entirety that can be defined, Freud referred to this as omnipotence of thoughts.[37]

By incorporating the linguistic perspective of opposites and the insight that what once was considered as magic, as history has shown, often turns into technical landmark innovations, the American physicist and philosopher David Bohm (1917–1992) explained that gifted individuals are able to think different thoughts because they can tolerate and intellectually capitalise on the ambivalence between opposites or two incompatible subjects by harmonising them. Bohm argued that the creative impulse in both art and science aims at "a certain oneness and totality, or wholeness, constituting a kind of harmony that is felt to be beautiful."[38]

The Danish physicist Niels Bohr (1885–1962) believed that if one could manage to cognitively hold abstract thought of an opposite nature together, then your thought would suspend pre-conceived thought patterns and allow for the mind to move to a new level. The consideration of seeking a unity, or wholeness, by bringing opposites together has not only been a preferred modus operandi in religious thought and physics but also in mathematics. The French philosopher of mathematics Albert Lautman (1908–1944) devoted much of his work on the examination of mathematical oppositions arguing convincingly that beyond the superficial appearances lay much more profound relationships. It has since been widely recognised that supposed mathematical oppositions are actually a force of tension within the same structural configuration and that it is from comprehending and elaborating on these tensions that creative advancements and paradigm shifts are likely to occur.[39]

The Hungarian-British author Arthur Koestler (1905–1983) published a highly praised work on creativity, *The Act of Creation* in 1964, where he distinguishes between creativity in divergent areas such as humour, science, and the arts. However, regardless of domain, Koestler argues that the essence of creativity is:

> ⋯ the perceiving of a situation or idea ⋯ in two self-consistent but habitually incompatible frames of reference.

He referred to this as *bisociation* and introduced matrices of thought to feature the process of bringing together two, or more, unrelated sets, often conventionally viewed as incompatible, even conflicting frames of thoughts, into a canvas of meaning. Koestler defined these matrices as "any ability, habit, or skill, any pattern of ordered behaviour governed by a 'code' of fixed rules." They could be developed by deploying tools such as comparisons, abstractions, categorisations, analogies, and metaphors. He broadly viewed "comparisons" as a type of bisociations and thus useful in the creative process.

According to Koestler, the matrices of thought could explain all types of creativity; in humour, the joke lies in the elimination of the expectation of a certain outcome within a certain matrix, hence along the awaited plot; however, the punch line abruptly replaces the expected outcome with an alternative one, hopefully releasing a comic effect. For the arts, Koestler argued that unrelated matrices are held in juxtaposition to one another, and the ability of experiencing art is to simultaneously acknowledge and sustain the aesthetically appealing perspectives of the matrices. For scientific breakthroughs, he claimed that these were achieved through the integration of two, or more, matrices into a larger synthesis, and the actual recognition of what up till then had been viewed as disconnected matrices were similar to the insights of the *Eureka* moments. Regardless of the types of creativity, they shared the following qualifying features:

- *economy*, Koestler refers to a sort of Occam's razor principle, where the interpolation, the extrapolation, or the transformation was left to the recipient, so as to fill in the gaps;
- *emphasis*, he argued that the focussed selection of relevant factors through simplification by removing non-essential items and an exaggeration of the important factors, all would help to develop matrices of thought; and
- *originality*, something akin to a surprise effect.

The fruitful combination of two seemingly incompatible matrices was according to Koestler enhanced through the relaxation, even the abandoning, of the deliberate rational thoughts that actively were working on solving the problem. By employing various techniques, trying to sidestep the automatic patterns of thought, these bisociative Eureka moments could be achieved. Through shifting the emphasis from what the key characteristics are in one matrix to a new perspective which might not be relevant for that particular matrix but fundamental for the integration with another matrix, the displacement of attention will allow for the discovery of hidden analogies. By drawing out the implicit axioms that formed the mental edifice for the old matrix, essentially it came down to perspective shifting. According to Koestler, this mental shift precedes the integration and establishment of a new matrix and to him the unconscious played a pivotal part in this process. So, for the artist, it came down to identify and represent these unarticulated connections between perceptions and manifest them as artworks that would resonate favourably with the audience.[40]

By describing and comparing different examples of creative work from different disciplines, Koestler concludes that they are bound together by the previously mentioned bisociations, through the blending of the elements borrowed from two previously unrelated matrices of thought into a new matrix of meaning. His fundamental idea is that any creative product is an act of bisociation, which goes beyond mere association of two, or several, apparently incompatible frames of thought. Koestler explains the breakthrough moment in science through the recognition when two previously disconnected matrices actually are compatible and can be amalgamated and form a new synthesis.[41]

Koestler recognised a distinction between bisociation and mere association, and the criteria for true creativity reflects that very difference:

The term 'bisociation' is meant to point to the independent, autonomous character of the matrices which are brought into contact in the creative act, whereas associative thought operates among members of a single pre-existing matrix.[42]

In examining "the criteria which distinguish bisociative originality from associative routine", Koestler highlighted the most important criteria:

> And this breakdown was not caused by establishing gradual, tentative connections between individual members of the separate matrices, but by the amalgamation of two realms as wholes, and the integration of the laws of both realms into a unified code of greater universality. Multiple discoveries and priority disputes do not diminish the objective, historical novelty produced by these bisociative events — they merely prove that the time was ripe for that particular synthesis.[43]

According to Koestler, many bisociative creative breakthroughs occur after a period of intense conscious effort directed at the goal or problem, in a period of relaxation when rational thought is abandoned, through various distractions such as dreams, in that sense it aligns with Wallas' creative process with its ensuing steps. Koestler argued that what holds back the capacity for creative activity is the tendency to fall back on automatic routines of thought and behaviour that often come to dominate individual's lives. So, the pattern underlying creativity is the perceiving of a situation in two (or more) self-consistent but habitually incompatible frames of reference. If and how these two intersect in a way that is recognised, bisociation has occurred. The exercise can help to identify the type of logic and what terms and framework that govern each matrix. Typically, this information exists implicitly, such as hidden axioms being taken for granted, which often is the constraint that prevents creative breakthroughs. He made the following observation:

> ...When two frames of reference have both become integrated into one it becomes difficult to imagine that previously they existed separately. The synthesis looks deceptively self-evident, and does not betray the imaginative effort needed to put its component parts together.[44]

This process can unfold in the following steps: determine the characteristics and nature of the frames of reference. Hence, it comes down to the discovery of hidden analogies and the bringing into consciousness of tacit axioms and habits of thought implied in the old matrix. As these are understood and deciphered into a shared jargon, a link which brings these previously incompatible frames of reference together will bisociate them on both mental planes. The final step is to define the character of the emotive charge and make an educated guess regarding the implicit elements that it may contain.

Koestler makes a distinction on how bisociation manifests in art versus science:

> The matrices with which the artist operates are chosen for their sensory qualities and emotive potential; his bisociative act is a juxtaposition of these planes or aspects of experience, not their fusion in an intellectual synthesis — to which, by their very nature, they do not lend themselves. This difference is reflected in the quasi-linear progression of science, compared with the quasi-timeless character of art, its continual re-statement of basic patterns of experience in changing idioms.[45]

Whereas for creative work in science, the bisociated matrices merge in a new synthesis, which in turn can merge with others on a higher level of the hierarchy, it becomes a process of successive confluences towards unitary and universal laws and structures.

Like Wallas and others, Koestler also acknowledged the role of the unconscious in the creative process, in fact to the degree that he acknowledged that conscious thought played only a minor role in the decisive bisociate phase. This unconscious guidance and inexplicable leaps of the imagination that eventually could trigger breakthrough intuitions became a key part in his theories. Koestler described it as a traffic of thoughts between the conscious and unconscious thought of mind, including an automisation of frequently performed actions which resulted in inflexible and stereotypical thought patterns. In reverse, thoughts and impressions travelling from the unconscious to the conscious which in contrast are more fluid and versatile in character and less perturbed by imprecision, inconsistencies, and contradictions. It is through this interchange that the incubation period, that in the best of times might lead to a bisociation, occurs, namely the activation of different matrices of thought in a flexible manner on different levels of consciousness.

However, what linguistic tool can be used to bring together opposite thoughts that might be tied together through some common denominator, however miniscule? Well, metaphors might serve that purpose.

In his book *On Creativity*, Bohm outlined a number of views on creativity where metaphors play an important part to help find a certain order in a chaotic environment and to bring the structure that can provide creative breakthroughs. Thus, by using known features metaphorically and trying to fit the unknown phenomena into this metaphorical order, and if that somehow can be intelligibly arranged, a creative breakthrough becomes a distinct possibility; however, in most cases, it is not sufficient to capture and adequately fathom that unknown.[46]

Metaphors might at first, and quite naturally so, be considered as belonging to poetry, magic language, and religious experiences as previously described. But also, cognitive science has taken an interest in how the mind structures thoughts, and it appears to have similarities with how the linguistic concept of metaphor works. The fundamental concept of this discipline rests on the assumption that "thinking can best be understood in terms of representational structures in the mind and computational procedures that operate on those structures". In the theory of situated cognition, the assumption is that our cognitive process does not only occur inside our brains but the world around us is also an integral part of our thinking, creating an "extended mind".[47,48,49]

The cognition is viewed to arise from the dynamic interaction between the brain, body, and the world that surrounds us, to some extent that the boundaries between mind, body, and world dissolve. That the cognition is situated means that it is also context-dependent, hence the cognitive activity cannot be separated from the situations in which it occurs. The specific thoughts cannot be understood if it is isolated from the individual and the contextual environment. In that sense, it becomes a valuable exercise to understand, mainly through writing, how humans have communicated throughout different time epochs. As such communication can be defined as an exchange of mental pictures between individuals. Language therefore acts as an important tool to symbolise and manifest thoughts.[50] And the symbolic language is a reference to our inner mental pictures that describe reality. That these differ over time is easily realised when reading older text and comparing their symbolic and figurative language with the current practices. Metaphors are perhaps one of the most common forms of symbolic language and play a central role in our thought process. In short, metaphors serve to describe the unknown or the abstract through the known. As the themes of metaphors trend, we can use these and what they sought to describe to fathom how our understanding of the world has altered over time. To conceptualise the unknown or the abstract, we need conceptual metaphors that somehow relate to the unknown. Koestler's concept of bisociation is apt in explaining how these might connect, also in the sense that it is not only a word-by-word exchange but a structural translation from one domain that is being transferred and maintained to another. Metaphoric reasoning thus means finding commonalities by highlighting ones considered important for connectivity and overseeing others. Without metaphors, abstract thinking would be challenging and therefore become an important part of developing new concepts. It becomes an exercise in finding a certain meaningful structure in chaos, through assigning concepts, categories, classes, and definitions from one knowledge domain to another as a starting point, and from there on creating a bespoke framework. It lays out boundaries that previously did not exist to us, and thereby it completes patterns previously incomplete and unknown.[51,52]

The types of metaphor themes are not only related to our physical experiences but also cultural, and the more layers of metaphors we deploy, the more abstract and culturally specific become the described phenomena or objects.[53]

That the unconscious applies categories to sort perceptions, and thus arrange and organise the association-based thinking, has been studied from many perspectives, among them empirical reviews of cultural stereotypes of people by ethnicity, age, and gender, indicating that this is done automatically and indeed unconsciously, the degree of categorisation is also not moderated through an individual's level of consciously explicit stereotyping. It appears to be a sorting mechanism that is innate. Hence, the associative aspect of the unconscious is girded through these categories.

These implicit cognitions are the sorting structures from the unconscious on knowledge, perceptions, and memory that influence behaviour and as such operate without our awareness thereof. An abstraction becomes a process that acts as a super-category denominator for all subordinate concepts and connects these into unified symmetry. The formation of conceptual abstractions can be arranged through the filtering of information, selecting an atom of common denominators drawn into a concept of observable phenomena. Abstraction is the opposite to specification, or asymmetry, which is the breaking down of general ideas into distinct particulars. An abstraction is thereby a process of compression, mapping multitudes of different data into a single data point, with properties that somehow are shared through similarities by each piece of associated data. Abstraction becomes an exercise in renouncing certain properties in an object or action and puts the emphasis on others and how that categorisation comes about depends on the unconscious structures. The abstraction process works as the symmetry forming of objects and actions.[54]

CONCLUSION

Albert Einstein was quoted saying: Combinatory play seems to be the essential feature in productive thought. However, the number of potential combinations can reach infinity, so the question remains, how do the gifted individuals arrive at value-added combinations? If we can define this component that helps select the promising combinations that can lead to a productive solution, and the source of its origins, it could be possible through artificial intelligence techniques, such as machine learning, to replicate this and start to automate the creative process. By identifying cues from a wide variety of subjects including religion, mysticism, various art forms, highlights from defining moments of enlightenment in the innovative process, show of a great similarity. Weird, even bizarre thoughts from the context of the reigning norms appear to precede artistic and innovative breakthroughs and the eureka moments of revelation arise through association-based free flow thinking where preconceived notions, stereotypes, and logic inferences are relaxed.

NOTES

1 Jung, Carl Gustav. *Man and His Symbols* (New York: Doubleday hardcover, 1964), p. 55.

2 Månsson, Lena. *Religiösa visioner och mystik erfarenhet* (Tidningen Kulturen, februari 9, 2009).

3 Kandinsky, Wassily, Sadler, M. T. (Translator), & Glew, Adrian (Editor). *Concerning the Spiritual in Art* (New York: MFA Publications and London: Tate Publishing, 2001).

4 Schmidhuber, Joergen. Developmental Robotics, Optimal Artificial Curiosity, Creativity, Music, and the Fine Arts *(Connection Science*, 18(2), 2006), pp. 173–187.

5 Orrell, David. *Truth or Beauty: Science and the Quest for Order* (New Haven: Yale University Press, 2012).

6 Sircello, Guy. *A New Theory of Beauty. Princeton Essays on the Arts*, 1 (Princeton, NJ: Princeton University Press, 1975).

7 Breton, André. *Manifestoes of Surrealism* (transl. Richard Seaver and Helen R. Lane, Ann Arbor: University of Michigan Press, 1971).

8 Neumann, Erich. *Art and the Creative Unconscious* (Princeton, NJ: Princeton University Press, 1974 edition).

9 Ibid.

10 Popper, Karl. *Objective Knowledge: An Evolutionary Approach* (Oxford: Oxford University Press, 1972), p. 70.

11 Forman, Robert K. *Mysticism* (Albany: State University of New York Press, 1999).

12 Paden, William E. Comparative Religion (In John Hinnells (Ed.), *The Routledge Companion to the Study of Religion*, Philadelphia, PA: Routledge, 2009), pp. 225–241.

13 McGinn, Bernard. *Mystical Union in Judaism, Christianity and Islam* (In Lindsay Jones (Ed.), *MacMillan Encyclopedia of Religion*, New York: MacMillan, 2005).

14 Einhorn, Stefan. *En dold Gud* (Stockholm, Sweden: Bokförlaget Forum, 1998).

15 Ibid.

16 Bassler, Jouette M. *The Parable of the Loaves* (*The Journal of Religion*, 66(2), April 1986), pp. 157–172.

17 Ibid.

18 Tillich, Paul J. Dynamics of Faith (Manhattan, NY: Harper & Row, 1957).

19 Mondin, Battista. Tillich's Doctrine of Religious Symbolism (*The Principle of Analogy in Protestant and Catholic Theology*, New York: Springer, 1963), pp. 118–146.

20 Tillich, Paul J. Dynamics of Faith (Manhattan, NY: Harper & Row, 1957).

21 Iser, Wolfgang. The Reading Process: A Phenomenological Approach (*New Literary History*, 3(2), On Interpretation: I, Winter 1972), p. 287.

22 Schwáb, Zoltán. Mind the Gap: The Impact of Wolfgang Iser's Reader-Response Criticism on Biblical Studies--A Critical Assessment (*Literature & Theology*, 17(2), Literary Hermeneutics, June 2003), p. 170.

23 Jung, C. G. On Psychic Energy (In *The Structure and Dynamics of the Psyche* (Collected Work of C.G. Jung), New York: Routledge, volume 8, 1970), paragraph 88.

24 Wright Buckham, John. The Mysticism of Plato (*The Open Court*, 1923(8), 1923), Article 2.

25 Otto, Rudolf. *The Idea of the Holy, An Inquiry into the Non-Rational Factor in the Idea of the Divine and Its Relation to the Rational* (Transl. of Das Heilige, Oxford: Oxford University Press, 1923).

26 James, William. *The Varieties of Religious Experience: A Study in Human Nature Being, the Gifford Lectures on Natural Religion Delivered at Edinburgh in 1901 - 1902* (London & Bombay: Longmans, Green, & Co, 1902).

27 Gill, Merton M. & Brenman, Margaret. *Hypnosis and Related States: Psychoanalytic Studies in Regression* (New York: International University Press, 1959), pp. 109–111.

28 Gimello, Robert M. *Mysticism and Meditation* (In 'Mysticism and Philosophical Analysis, Katz Steven T. (ed), London: Oxford University Press, 1978), pp. 170–199.

29 Arieti, Silvano. *Creativity: The Magic Synthesis* (New York: Diane Pub Co, 1976), p. 13.

30 Batson, C. Daniel & Ventis, W. L. *The Religious Experience: A Social-Psychological Perspective* (Oxford: Oxford University Press, Paperback 1982).

31 Deikman, A. J. Bimodal Consciousness (*Archives of General Psychiatry*, 25, 1971), pp. 481–489.

32 Deikman, A. J. Deautomatization and the Mystic Experience (*Psychiatry*, 29, 1966), p. 337 onwards.

33 Gill, Merton M. & Brenman, Margaret. *Hypnosis and Related States: Psychoanalytic Studies in Regression* (New York: International University Press, 1959), p. 178.

34 Arieti, Silvano. *Creativity: The Magic Synthesis* (New York: Diane Pub Co, 1976), p. 83 onwards.

35 Malinowski, Bronisław. *Magic, Science and Religion and Other Essays* (Glencoe, IL: The Free Press, 1948).

36 Ogden, Charles Kay & Richards, Ivor. A. *The Meaning of Meaning: A Study of the Influence of Language upon Thought and of the Science of Symbolism* (Eastford, CT: Martino Fine Book, 2013, original 1923).

37 Freud, Sigmund. *Totem and Taboo: Resemblances Between the Mental Lives of Savages and Neurotics* (Mineola, NY: Dover Publications, 2011, original translation 1918).

38 Bohm, David. *On Creativity* (Philadelphia, PA: Routledge Classic, 2nd edition, 1998).

39 Lautman, Albert. *Mathematics, Ideas, and the Physical Real* (Mathématiques, les idées et le réel physique, 1938, translated by Simon B. Duffy, New York: Continuum International Publishing Group, 2011).

40 Koestler, Arthur. *The Act of Creation* (London, UK: Hutchinson & Co, 1964).

41 Ibid.

42 Ibid.

43 Ibid.

44 Ibid.

45 Ibid.

46 Bohm, David. On Creativity (Philadelphia, PA: Routledge Classic, 2nd edition, 1998).

47 Miller, G. A. The Cognitive Revolution: A Historical Perspective (Trends in Cognitive Sciences, 7(3), 2003), pp. 141–144.

48 Clark, Andy & Chalmers, David. The Extended Mind (Analysis, 58(1), January 1998), pp. 7–19.

49 Clark, Andy. Being There: Putting Brain, Body, and World Together Again (Cambridge, MA: Bradford Books, 1998).

50 Taylor, John R. Cognitive Grammar (Oxford: Oxford University Press, 2002), p. 30.

51 Lakoff, George & Johnson, Mark. Metaphors We Live By (Chicago, IL: University of Chicago Press, 1st edition, 2003).

52 Lakoff, George & Johnson, Mark. Philosophy in the Flesh: The Embodied Mind and Its Challenge to Western Thought (New York: Basic Books, 1999).

53 Danesi, Marcel. The Dimensionality of Metaphor (Sign Systems Studies, 27, 1999), pp. 60–87.

54 Perruchet, P., Gallego, J., & Savy, I. A Critical Reappraisal of the Evidence for Unconscious Abstraction of Deterministic Rules in Complex Experimental Situations (Cognitive Psychology, 22(4), October 1990), pp. 493–516.

4

COMPUTATIONAL CREATIVITY

...the ghost in the machine...

Gilbert Ryle, British philosopher (1900–1976),
The Concept of Mind.

This chapter on computational creativity is best introduced through a recap from the preceding chapters that took a wide-ranging explorative tour in the world of creativity. Thus, it deliberately examined many perspectives to fathom whether the creative process can be comprehensively understood in the quest to articulate a blueprint with the aspiration of achieving computational creativity. In Chapter 1, Wallas' creative process was outlined with its four ensuing steps: preparation, incubation, illumination, and verification. Despite now being almost a century old, most creative researchers do concur with Wallas' theory, where it is the incubation phase that occasionally leads to illumination that remains the least understood and is the area where artificial intelligence potentially could augment human creative endeavours. In Chapter 2, the role of the unconscious part of the human mind in triggering innovative new ideas was discussed, where concepts such as intuition and insight were delineated and theories on how the unconscious actually operates elaborated on. Then in Chapter 3, a broad range of disciplines were dissected from the creative perspective with some captivating aspects emerging. In the world of art, attempts to depict the unspoken have often proven to be the key in

DOI: 10.1201/9781003194941-5

producing master pieces, technical abilities aside. For religious mystical experiences, the main challenge for theologians has been to find means to describe what appear as divine acts in a comprehensive manner where the switch between different worlds, rational and the seemingly irrational, is an important part of such experiences. In linguistics and literature, different techniques have evolved to creatively describe phenomena, esoteric, and others, where conventional language has not really sufficed. The author Arthur Koestler introduced a generic method, labelled bisociation, where finding a common denominator between contrasting aspects, however miniscule, could provide the illuminating insight. However, it is still not a mundane exercise as these common denominators often have proven to be of an unconscious nature and hence it explains the relatively rare occurrences of creative breakthroughs, as it is only occasionally that they will transcend into our awareness. Finding a union in opposites, subtly apparent in the tension between incompatible subjects, and through the acknowledgement of unconscious influences, seem across disciplines to point to an approach that facilitates the incubation phase of the creative process. A certain amount of aesthetic elegance appears to define value-adding solutions, this as symmetry is found amongst perceived chaos and previously not conjoined asymmetric structures.

This provides a valuable clue in how to identify creative solutions amongst a myriad of potential alternatives, such as the search of a symmetric (aesthetic) order integrating two structures, or knowledge domains, through a common denominator. Analogies, conceptualisations, and metaphors serve as good examples here, where known themes or structures are deployed to describe unknown such, but they only tend to work if the relationship between the known and unknown can be symmetrically aligned through some shared characteristics, often of an unrecognised nature. And indeed, creative individuals throughout history testify that often the revelation of the innovative sort came in a graphical format before it could be articulated in words. However, to capture and replicate unconscious thought processes that are so pivotal for creative breakthroughs into formal rules, do require a paradigm shift in artificial intelligence in general, and computational creativity in particular. Thus, it is an undertaking that requires an unconventional approach to modelling, which is what this concluding chapter is about. Computational creativity is for the purpose of this book defined as algorithms, or other computer code, replicating the human creative process, or parts thereof.

But the progress in achieving computational creativity has so far been modest, where part of the problem lies in the understanding of creativity itself. Some of the considerations are of a philosophical nature, such as if an algorithm is able to produce creative thoughts, of any sort, should that be attributed to the algorithm or the programmer responsible for developing it? Other issues are more pragmatical, how do we rank and rate creative solutions? Other issues relate to the data, and as an algorithm is dependent on the exactness and precision of its inputs. And if these have been too loosely formulated, any output will subsequently therefore suffer, so we cannot expect the flexibility that we humans are equipped with going back and forth altering and fine-tuning assumptions. And as has been discussed in previous chapters, creativity is about breaking rules, how do we go about developing code that break rules, as it by default is hardcoded to follow rules. If a program can only do what it was programmed to do, can that by definition be considered as creativity?

Perhaps as a more practical way to circumvent these more definitional ponderings, and still ensuring that computational creativity provides valuable perspectives, a viable approach would instead seek where artificial intelligence can optimise the man–machine connection in the creative process. So, what it is that artificial intelligence currently could do in the development of computational creativity? At first, let us highlight some of the limitations of artificial intelligence in this regard.

The process of creativity with a view to produce new innovative thinking often differs from traditional problem-solving given its complexity; it typically lacks an *exact* solution that in advance is known, and the problem in itself is usually never that specifically defined, given the many unknown factors. The problem with deploying artificial intelligence in a search for a 'correct' solution to a scientific conundrum, is that it lacks the capability of interpreting the association-based blended scenarios it has been coded to generate and link these with a potential solution. In short, the absence of an imaginative coherence prevents it from finding a potentially value-adding solution and thus it will never stop generating scenarios and could keep going *ad infinitum*. In contrast, our human intelligence can experience a eureka moment once it realises a correct solution out of the iterative generation of scenarios, of which most are chaotic and erratic and out of no value, and then stops to proceed to evaluation and verification. From the human perspective, this iterative process arranges the search by narrowing down the key determinants, and a potentially correct path often being acknowledged by subjective feel-good factors, and hence as the next step, start to home in on that particular path in search for a conclusion. It would be difficult to develop an artificial intelligence tool to function in such manner, but rather it keeps generating scenarios across the line, as it cannot capture the dynamic reinforcement mechanism and feedback loops. However, artificial intelligence can augment the incubation phase as the normal protocol for experimental testing typically only includes variations within the pre-set assumptions and context, part or wholly random test scenarios are rarely included and if so, lacks guidance but as historical hindsight shows it is in that realm that scientific breakthroughs often occur.

At the heart of amalgamating artificial intelligence with human intelligence lies the ability to produce conceptual change by applying imagination to a set problem through distorting some of the objects and relationships as a mean to purposely skew the mental representation to reach a higher representation of reality. This by allowing for an artificial intelligence tool to randomly generate scenarios, in accordance with parameters set by human intelligence at onset, and by allowing for human intelligence to select promising scenarios for further narrowing down of paths with a view of identifying viable solutions. The power of artificial intelligence in this context therefore lies in;

- in its scenario generating capacity, which exceeds that of what humans are capable of, and;
- its ability to create random scenarios, even such of a bizarre nature, supersedes that of human imagination.

Hence, artificial intelligence and natural intelligence needs to work hand in hand, in solving problems of an open-ended nature. As the process of creativity follows generic phases, it allows for an agnostic dynamic model to be developed. Figure 4.1 details the blueprint and highlights the various phases, where a mixture of thought structures are involved. At the set-up in the preparation phase, which exclusively is a domain for the human intelligence, the problem must be defined, and assumptions and key inputs are determined. These input parameters form the building blocks to produce an abstract mental representation that constitutes the basis to generate scenarios in the incubation phase. The incubation phase draws a lot on the seemingly irrational associations that are made in the unconscious part of the mind in order to break the mental block that prevents creative thinking, it is limited by the capacity of human imagination and the level of subject matter expertise. Scientific breakthroughs often appear outside the realms of what is considered rational, so irrationality can loosely be equivalent of chaotic associations. But the association-based thinking, albeit irrational, must still follow a suite of rules, so that an artificial intelligence scenario generator tool is able to alter meanings and shift perspectives, and is well suited for both figurative- and text-based categories. Obviously, an algorithm will indiscriminately create scenarios, and a large number of nonsense is expected to be generated. Hence, human intervention is required to step in and order these scenarios, by selecting promising ones for further elaboration as new parameters are identified and fed back, or progress to verification to ascertain their eligibility as proper solutions. This feedback and verification loop, set to repeat until a successful solution is found, is again an exclusive domain of human intelligence.

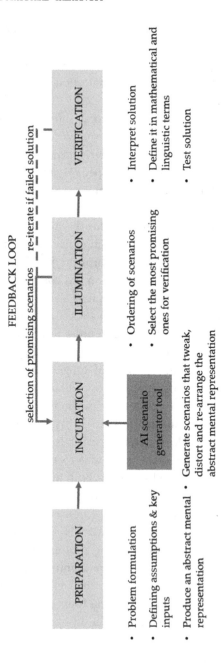

Figure 4.1 A graphic depiction of how an artificial intelligence scenario generator tool supports the process of creativity.

So, how are then these scenarios generated? A promising approach, mimicking several characteristics of Koestler's bisociation concept, is conceptual blending. As its name alludes, it is based on the assumption that all new knowledge originates out of a blend from existing knowledge domains. Hence, by applying known structures in a mixing and matching approach, sometimes randomly such as the serendipitous moments can highlight, and in other instances through deliberate trial-and-error experimentation. The purpose of conceptual blending is explained as:

> ...conceptual blending combines the smoothness of metaphor with the structural complexity and organizing power of analogy. We can think of blending as a cognitive operation in which conceptual ingredients do not flow in a single direction, but are thoroughly stirred together, to create a new structure with its own emergent meanings.[1,2]

The components of a blending process consist of:

- at a minimum two *knowledge spaces*, which include the contents of a specific situation or idea and form the foundation of the blending;
- a *generic space* which captures a common structure which is present in all input spaces;
- a *blend space* in which a selected projection of elements from the knowledge spaces are combined with a general structure from the generic space; inferences arising from these combinations reside here, sometimes leading to emergent structures that contradict with the inputs from the knowledge spaces; and
- cross-space mapping of counterparts represents various types of connections, such as connections similar to metaphors, between corresponding structures in the input spaces.[3,4]

Obviously, a blending process will generate a huge number of scenarios through different combinations of amalgamating knowledge spaces, so optimisation principles have been presented to help narrow down the selection towards the ones considered most value-adding. This is typically done through ascertaining consistency and by applying metrics that evaluates their 'quality', however such an inspection can only partially be automated, and require a manual review, which makes such an exercise onerous and time consuming, and prone to human errors. It is of importance to understand that the actual blend of knowledge spaces need not to neither be the intersection nor the union thereof but are typically selected parts bound together through a shared structure, and the other parts are omitted from the blend. An emergent structure can be added in the blend which is then not directly provided from the input knowledge spaces but forms through three processes:

1 composition, which brings the elements from the knowledge spaces together to create new relations that did not exist in the individual knowledge spaces;

2 completion, means the inference of additional information that originates from insights gained through the actual blending; and

3 elaboration, short for running the blend, meaning that proactive work is conducted based on the interacting behaviour of the selected elements in the blend with a view of identifying creative value-added logic or concepts.

The conceptual blend theory is attractive in that it tallies many of the key features of the creative process that have been acknowledged through the wide spectra of disciplines that have formed their own view on how creativity works. Yet, the practical applications of the conceptual blend theory have so far been few, as some hurdles have been left basically unanswered, the main ones being:

1 How do we know which knowledge domains to load up as part of the input, and what should they look like? From history we do know that it is some unlikely knowledge combinations that can trigger the inspiration to creative breakthroughs.

2 The unconscious plays an important role, and the common denominator that often binds together disparate, even contrasting knowledge structure, resides there. But how can we, or an artificial intelligence algorithm, identify something we are not even aware of? It appears that without acknowledging and articulating implicit unconscious assumptions, a conceptual blending technique is bound to only partially function. Thus, there is a step that must precede the preparation of knowledge spaces, namely the recognition of the 'unspoken', to this there is a useful contraption that can be utilised and will be presented below.

3 And, finally, can evaluation be automated, as otherwise the manual review can easily become overwhelming. From the review of creativity from various disciplines, many artists and innovators testify to that insights hold a certain amount of aesthetic qualities, to be interpreted in its broadest sense, where out a chaos and asymmetry, symmetric patterns suddenly emerge and where the solution often lies. If this is possible to automate, it would speed up the creative process considerably.

DEVELOPING A BLUEPRINT FOR COMPUTATIONAL CREATIVITY

By deploying the conceptual blend theory, with its pedigree from a raft of ideas on creativity, as the edifice and by adequately addressing some of its shortcoming highlighted through the above stated questions, a blueprint for computational creativity can be graphically expressed which lends itself for the design of generic applications.

To start with, how do we know what knowledge domains to load as input, as history has proven that the inspiration to innovative breakthroughs could come from any of a broad variety of disciplines?

In all, a knowledge space acts as a vessel for subject matter expertise delineated through framework, idiosyncratic concepts, terminology, formulae, models, basically what serves as the building blocks for knowledge. The selection of knowledge domains needs to be separated in two groupings, the host space whether that be a particular discipline within science, a particular art genre, or similarly which is wherein new innovative concepts are sought, and all the others. By rearranging, blending, and combining the host space with the other knowledge structures, in a systematic mean through one-by-one testing, the aspiration is to allow for value-added insights to emerge. Hence, a relatively straightforward procedure, but against which knowledge areas should the host space be blended?

Perhaps surprisingly to many, the universe of knowledge is fairly limited and is structured and arranged in forms that lend itself for comparative analysis. Albeit no doubt the knowledge spaces are too extensive for most single individuals to absorb, hence it explains why the number of universal geniuses appear so far and few between. To be noted, it is not an encyclopedic database that is required in the knowledge spaces, but rather how each knowledge domain is structured, for both the generic and idiosyncratic elements. The list of academic fields and their structure provide a comprehensive universe of knowledge domains and one categorisation, to which there are sub-categories, can be outlined as:

- humanities
  - history
  - languages and literature
  - law
  - performing arts
  - philosophy
  - theology
  - visual arts
- social sciences
  - anthropology
  - economics
  - geography
  - political science
  - psychology
  - sociology
  - social work

- natural sciences
  - astronomy
  - biology
  - chemistry
  - geology
  - physics
- formal sciences
  - computer science
  - mathematics
- applied sciences
  - business administration
  - engineering and technology
  - medicine

Whilst the classification of knowledge for each of these academic disciplines follows structures that allow for codification, one of the most important features is overlooked. Creative researchers have provided clues on where to look for potential connections. Henri Poincaré argued that "Among chosen combinations the most fertile will often be those formed of elements drawn from domains which are far apart."[5] Hence, seeking to note identity in difference from knowledge domains not obviously linked is a starting point to provide new innovative perspectives of a serendipitous nature. Often it is the same source that triggers the ambiguity and connects seemingly independent elements.

But as previously noted, the common denominators that at times bind even disparate knowledge structures together and trigger a new set of knowledge tend to reside in the unconscious, which explains why they are so difficult to identify. Therefore, blending from this perspective can be viewed as a compression where two or more knowledge structures are consolidated into a single blend structure, and it targets the conceptual relations, but these are often the implicit and unassumed ones. So, to make use of these in the conceptual blend model, they first have to be articulated, which explains why the conceptual blending theory, despite its sound assumptions in other areas, has had little success in any practical use, as it does not incorporate unconscious knowledge and assumptions.

The Polish-American philosopher Alfred Korzybski (1879–1950) developed a scientific approach labelled *general semantics* aimed to provide a better understanding of how we describe objects and phenomena in the world by recognising the limiting structure of language. He referred to these as *silent presuppositions*, or undefined terms, which have by many been pointed out as a significant problem, in particular in science, where an assumed exactness is often blurred through a number of implicit assumptions.[6] Korzybski argued that:

> ... when we 'think' without words, or in pictures or visualizations (which involve structure and, therefore, relations), we may discover new aspects and relations on silent levels, and so may formulate important theoretical results in the general search for a similarity of structure between the two levels, silent and verbal. Practically all important advances are made in that way.[7]

According to Korzybski, it is our language that through its restrictive structure forces us to sort, select, and generalise phenomena in the world, and this by default means that we have to omit certain features, and over time they become silent presuppositions. He defined this language structure as 'a complex of ordered and interrelated parts', with the parts acting to distinguish objects by classifying them according to common, but generally not individual, characteristics. He divided words into two categories: descriptive words and inferential words, and in science both these types are used, descriptive observations and then the exercise to formulate generalised rules about these observations. Hence, the descriptive type named characteristics and their relational terms reflecting actual experiences, and at the other level, the inferential words that provide a colloquial on how to refer to these direct experiences, thus the generalisation. Abstraction and generalisation therefore exclude most of the characteristics that do not form part of the shared features. The power of good science then rests in that it is able to develop and articulate a language capable of linking generalisations in a meticulously arranged hierarchy so that these at different levels become coherent, however with the downside that at every move up in the hierarchy, additional descriptions must be dropped. In essence, it is detaching itself further and further away from reality, hereby losing features that potentially could form common denominators between knowledge domains. To this point, the American academic S.I. Hayakawa (1906–1992) aptly commented that:

> When a scientist 'understands' he has "ordered his observations at the objective, descriptive, and higher inferential levels of abstraction into a workable system in which all levels are related to other levels in terms of a few, powerful, generalization.[8]

Herein lies the problem that Korzybski identified with generalisation, which is that the further along the hierarchy you go, the greater the distance one gets from the original, first order, experience. It becomes ever more abstract and the description of reality loses its concreteness, and the major problem with this process is that we eventually tend to think that the words themselves equal reality.[9] To this end, Korzybski designed a contraption to highlight and address this structural differential. For reasons of pedagogy, Korzybski considered that an understanding of structural differentials required visualisation. The contraption seeks to produce more efficient forms of thought, highlighting the actual forms, functions, or contents of the object it was set to describe, thereby providing a more comprehensive understanding. The visualisation allowed for a facilitated moving around within the structural hierarchy and a facility to remove false assumptions and enable the recognition of silent presuppositions. He used it, in education amongst others, to demonstrate that human beings abstract reality, and that verbal abstractions build on themselves indefinitely through many levels by being chained in order. Through visualising the relationship between language and the phenomena or object it seeks to describe, the implicit gaps become apparent and helps to clarify what is in fact not there. Korzybski commented, much in concurrence with other theories on creativity, that the talent for creative insight came in the ability to readily be able to cognitively move between different levels of abstraction in the knowledge structure and understanding where the silent presuppositions reside and being able to articulate them.[10]

Given that the focus of finding a creative solution should be if and how the unconscious and implicit elements of the knowledge structures act as connecting bridges and once these have been illuminated, the count and ranking of such would serve as a first sorting mechanism, which in effect would filter down the number of scenarios considerably. This will constitute an evaluative filter capable of only allowing blend scenarios with either common denominators that only occur through this systematic acknowledgement and then provides a broader spectra of potential connects. This is facilitated as the ones previously deemed as unspoken are marked as such and given a higher value in the ranking of connects. Also, the evaluation is augmented if it is goal seeking, such that the end solution can be articulated at a high level at least. This is in particular where machine learning will greatly facilitate the creative process, as through the mass generation of blended scenarios, in particular drawing out any of a serendipitous nature, it will start to identify those potentially value-adding and put them forward for a more in-depth human inspection. The ranking and sorting of the many generated scenarios against certain set design parameters, such as symmetry and aesthetics, however defined, are where artificial intelligence can provide excellent tools to speed up and systematise the process.

How are then these silent presuppositions made to emerge and become visible? Korzybski's contraption, which he labelled anthropometer, was developed to highlight this structural differential, and it consisted of three basic objects with a view of presenting what is missing, and making a distinction between events, objects, and labels. Thus, the anthropometer is a visualisation tool. In Figure 4.2, the parabola-like figure represents events, which is a phenomenon or object beyond our direct observation, a world known to us only inferentially, consisting of innumerable characteristics or events, at

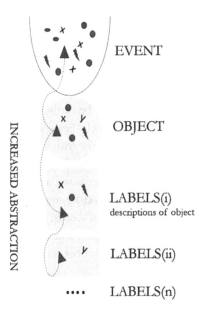

Figure 4.2 The visualisation of characteristics included and omitted as part of the abstraction process of an object.

macro and micro levels. Per definition, an event can extend indefinitely, in the way it can be described through more details. The event level represents the raw data from which we abstract and is the typical focus of study for science, including atoms, particles, cells, electrons, and the likes. In short, it is the event level we abstract from. The event level also includes details that we do not abstract or simply cannot abstract. Hence, only certain of these characteristics connect with the next level and have abstracted a particular set of characteristics from all possible characteristics of the events. The next level is the object, and here a structural difference can be made based on whether an object connects to the higher level event or not. Such an object is an abstraction of the event, and the number of connects represents its perceived characteristics that define this abstraction. Connects that are not chained to an object are subsequently the unperceived characteristics.

Some of the connects of the object do not correspond to characteristics of the event, indicating that those are added by our cognitive and perceptual processes. The next order of abstraction are the labels, as we associate the data with a word or label, being the first level of verbal awareness. They are descriptive, including naming the characteristics of the object, and they can be further generalised and broken down into additional levels of labels. From the descriptive level, the verbal abstracting process proceeds with additional inference that can continue indefinitely. Through this delineation, Korzybski sought to make a point of that what is perceived a correct deductive scientific reasoning of conscious abstracting, might bring the realisation that verbal articulations in forms of words, names, and labels, do not cover all characteristics of an object, and that the characteristics of the object are not the same in number and quality as those of the event.

This as the characteristics of the inputs need not to be the same in number and quality as those of the solution that they seek to produce (Figure 4.3).

CONCLUDING THOUGHTS

Perhaps it is so that we humans put too much hope in the "ghost in the machine", the expectation that some artificial intelligence application will be able to vastly improve our creative ability. Even if we have developed algorithms capable of computational creativity, there is so much more to the innovative process than merely coming up with brilliant innovative ideas, there are impediments of a psychological and sociological nature that can, for a while at least, block drastic changes to the status quo. History is full of misunderstood genius whose ideas arrived "too early", which is supposed to mean that mainstream society, but also most of the elite and avant-garde artist and scientist communities, where far too mentally and intellectually chained to the existing dogmas and narratives to see beyond these boundaries. They simply, even if recognising the merits of new ideas, had too much vested interests in the old ones as their careers

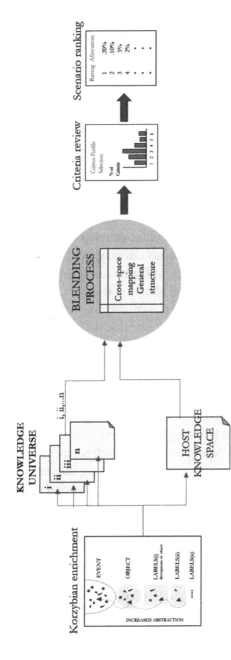

Figure 4.3 The process of conceptual blending, enriched through Korzybian analysis and criteria ranked evaluation

were built on these. And as any psychologist will tell you, embracing the new comes with a certain baldness and risk willing attitude that most people just are not equipped with, swimming with the tide rather than against it is the preferred modus operandi. New ideas breaking with existing dogmas were seen as threatening, and if at all formally acknowledged, then often ridiculed, to the extent that sometimes its originator risked ostracisation, and in certain times and cultures, even prison sentences or worse. As new innovative ideas often are in quite stark contrast with how things are supposed to be, they can be seen so unfathomable that they become hard to relate to and therefore embrace. What then if a machine starts to generate creative solutions that even the most well-meaning artists and scientists will have difficulties grasping, as they might be too ingenious for what we humans can grasp. Will we even be able to recognise them? It certainly will take some leaps of faith in trusting what machines can and will be able to create.

Arthur Koestler and others were certainly onto something when they made a point of making sure that the unspoken was brought to our attention as a mean to enlighten us. These implicit factors often block our thought processes to see things for what they are, namely the full spectra of characteristics of the underlying phenomena. Realising the limitations of the words that our narrated language provide is where artificial intelligence in a systematic manner can help us considerably as the proverbial eye-opener in providing fresh perspectives and be the trigger that ignites value-added solutions. Because, it is when we can depict something that we can put words to it, so it is not by chance that many groundbreaking ideas first sprang out of our minds in the form of graphical representations before they could be articulated in words and formulae, at times a whole new vocabulary had to be introduced, often borrowed from another knowledge domain.

Hence, when engaging in the exciting work of innovation and the exploration on how artificial intelligence could enhance the creative process, let us not forget the lessons from history, that truly innovative ideas are often at first meet with resistance as they are not understood by most contemporary, preferring to stick to the tried and tested. In the end, it still will be us humans that simultaneously will be both the friend and foe of innovative thinking, a psychological insight to which artificial intelligence might not be able to do much about.

NOTES

1   Veale, T. & Donoghue, D. O. Computation and Blending (*Cognitive Linguistics*, 11(3–4), 2000), pp. 253–282.

2   Fauconnier, Gilles & Turner, Mark. *The Way We Think: Conceptual Blending and the Mind's Hidden Complexities* (New York: Basic Books, 2008).

3   Fauconnier, Gilles & Turner, Mark. Conceptual Integration Networks (*Cognitive Science*, 22(2), 1998), pp. 133–187.

4   Fauconnier, Gilles & Turner, Mark. Conceptual Blending, Form and Meaning (*Recherches En Communication*, 2003).

5   Dennett, Daniel C. *Brainstorms: Philosophical Essays on Mind and Psychology* (The MIT Press, 1978), p. 80.

6   Korzybski, Alfred. *Science and Sanity: An Introduction to Non-Aristotelian Systems and General Semantics* (New York: Institute of General Semantics, 5th edition, 1994).

7   Korzybski, Alfred. *Collected Writings 1920-1950* (New York: Institute of General Semantics, 1990), p. 690.

8   Hayakawa, S. I. *Language in Thought and Action* (San Diego, CA: Harcourt Brace & World, 2nd edition, 1964), p. 154.

9   Korzybski, Alfred. *Science and Sanity: An Introduction to Non-Aristotelian Systems and General Semantics* (New York: Institute of General Semantics, 5th edition, 1994).

10 Ibid.

REFERENCES

Adler, Alfred. *The Individual Psychology of Alfred Adler* (New York: Harper Torchbooks, 1964).

Albert, R.S. & Runco, M.A. A History of Research on Creativity (In R.J. Sternberg (Ed.), *Handbook of Creativity*, Cambridge: Cambridge University Press, 1999), p. 5.

American Psychiatric Association. *DSM-5 Update: Supplement to Diagnostic and Statistical Manual of Mental Disorders* (Philadelphia, PA: American Psychiatric Association Publishing, 5th edition, 2016).

Arieti, Silvano. *Creativity: The Magic Synthesis* (New York: Diane Pub Co, 1976).

Baas, Matthijs, De Dreu Carsten, K.W., & Nijstad, Bernard A. A Meta-Analysis of 25 Years of Mood-Creativity Research: Hedonic Tone, Activation, or Regulatory Focus? (*Psychological Bulletin*, 134(6), November 2008), pp. 779–806.

Bailin, Sharon. Critical and Creative Thinking (*Informal Logic*, 9(1), 1987), pp. 23–30.

Bassler, Jouette M. The Parable of the Loaves (*The Journal of Religion*, 66(2), April 1986), pp. 157–172.

Batson, C. Daniel & Ventis, W.L. *The Religious Experience: A Social-Psychological Perspective* (Oxford: Oxford University Press, Paperback 1982).

Boden, Margret, A. *The Creative Mind: Myths and Mechanisms* (London, UK: Routledge, 2004).

Bohm, David. *On Creativity* (New York: Routledge Classic, 2nd edition, 1998).

Breton, André. *Manifestoes of Surrealism* (transl. Richard Seaver and Helen R. Lane, Ann Arbor: University of Michigan Press, 1971).

Claridge, G. & Blakey, S. Schizotypy and Affective Temperament: Relationships with Divergent Thinking and Creativity Styles (*Personality and Individual Differences*, 46(8), 2009), pp. 820–826.

Clark, Andy. *Being There: Putting Brain, Body, and World Together Again* (Cambridge, MA: Bradford Books, 1998).

Clark, Andy & Chalmers, David. The Extended Mind (*Analysis*, 58(1), January 1998), pp. 7–19.

Claxton, G.L. Investigating Human Intuition: Knowing Without Knowing Why (*Psychologist*, 11(5), 1998), pp. 217–220.

Cropley, D.H., Kaufman, J.C., & Cropley, A.J. Malevolent Creativity: A Functional Model of Creativity in Terrorism and Crime (*Creativity Research Journal*, 20, April 2008), pp. 105–115.

Csikszentmihályi, Mihaly. *Flow: The Psychology of Optimal Experience* (New York: Harper & Row, 1990).

Csikszentmihályi, Mihaly. *Handbook of Creativity* (Edited extract from R. Sternberg (Ed.), Cambridge: Cambridge University Press, 1990).

Danesi, Marcel. The Dimensionality of Metaphor (*Sign Systems Studies*, 27, 1999), pp. 60–87.

Davis, Mark A. Understanding the Relationship between Mood and Creativity: A Meta-Analysis (*Organizational Behavior and Human Decision Processes*, 100(1), January 2009), pp. 25–38.

De Bono, Edward. *Lateral Thinking: Creativity Step by Step* (New York: Harper & Row, 1970).

de Manzano, Ö., Cervenka, S., Karabanov, A., Farde, L., & Ullén, F. *Samband mellan psykisk ohälsa och kreativitet*, 2010. https://ki.se/nyheter/samband-mellan-psykisk-ohalsa-och-kreativitet (accessed 1 April 2021)

Deikman, A.J. Deautomatization and the Mystic Experience (*Psychiatry*, 29, 1966), p. 337.

Deikman, A.J. Bimodal Consciousness (*Archives of General Psychiatry*, 25, 1971), pp. 481–489.

Dijksterhuis, A. & Nordgren, L.F. A Theory of Unconscious Thought Perspectives (*Psychological Science*, 1(2), June 2006), pp. 95–109.

Einhorn, Stefan. *En dold Gud* (Stockholm, Sweden: Bokförlaget Forum, 1998).

Fauconnier, Gilles & Turner, Mark. Conceptual Integration Networks (*Cognitive Science*, 22(2), 1998), 133–187.

Fauconnier, Gilles & Turner, Mark. Conceptual Blending, Form and Meaning (*Recherches En Communication*, 2003).

Fauconnier, Gilles & Turner, Mark. *The Way We Think: Conceptual Blending and the Mind's Hidden Complexities* (New York: Basic Books, 2008).

Fazel, Seena, Goodwin, Guy M., Grann, Martin, Lichtenstein, Paul, & Lång- ström, Niklas. Bipolar Disorder and Violent Crime: New Evidence from Population-Based Longitudinal Studies and Systematic Review (*Archives of General Psychiatry*, 67, September 7, 2010), pp. 931–938.

Forman, Robert K. Mysticism (Albany: State University of New York Press, 1999).

Freud, Sigmund. *Totem and Taboo: Resemblances between the Mental Lives of Savages and Neu- rotics* (Mineola, NY: Dover Publications, 2011, original translation 1918).

Frey, Angelica. *A New Account of Robert Lowell's Mania Risks Glorifying It* (Hyperallergic, May 3, 2017).

Furnham, Batey M. The Relationship between Creativity, Schizotypy and Intelli- gence (*Individual Differences Research*, 7, 2009), pp. 272–284.

Furnham, Batey M., Anand, K., & Manfield, J. Personality, Hypomania, Intel- ligence and Creativity (*Personality and Individual Differences*, 44(5), 2008), pp. 1060–1069.

Gigerenzer, G. Why Heuristics Work (*Perspectives on Psychological Science*, 3(1), Janu- ary 1, 2008), pp. 20–29.

Gigerenzer, G. & Selten, R. (Eds). *Bounded Rationality: The Adaptive Toolbox* (Cambridge: MIT Press, 2001).

Gilhooly, Kenneth J. Incubation and Intuition in Creative Problem Solving (*Frontiers in Psychology*, 7, 2016), p. 1076.

Gill, Merton M., & Brenman, Margaret. *Hypnosis and Related States: Psychoanalytic Studies in Regression* (New York: International University Press, 1959).

Gimello, Robert M. Mysticism and Meditation (In Steven T. Katz (Ed.), *Mysti- cism and Philosophical Analysis*, London: Oxford University Press, 1978), pp. 170–199.

Gino, Francesca & Wiltermuth, Scott S. Evil Genius? How Dishonesty Can Lead to Greater Creativity (*Psychological Science*, 25, February 18, 2014), pp. 973–981.

Goodwin, Frederick K. & Redfield Jamison, Kay. *Manic-Depressive Illness - Bipolar Dis- orders and Recurrent Depression* (New York: Oxford University Press, 95, 2007).

Guilford, J.P. Creativity (*American Psychologist*, 5(9), 1950), pp. 677–688.

Guilford, J.P. Creativity: Yesterday, Today and Tomorrow (*Journal of Creative Behavior*, 1, Winter 1967), pp. 3–14.

Hadamard, Jacques. The Psychology of Invention in the Mathematical Field (*Philosophy and Phenomenological Research*, 10(2), 1949), pp. 288–289.

Hayakawa, S.I. *Language in Thought and Action* (San Diego, CA: Harcourt Brace & World, 2nd edition, 1964).

Hélie, S. & Sun, R. Incubation, Insight, and Creative Problem Solving: A Unified Theory and a Connectionist Model (*Psychological Review*, 117(3), 2010), pp. 994–1024.

Iser, Wolfgang. The Reading Process: a Phenomenological Approach (*New Literary History*, 3(2), On Interpretation: I, Winter 1972), p. 287.

James, William. *The Varieties of Religious Experience: A Study in Human Nature Being, the Gifford Lectures on Natural Religion Delivered at Edinburgh in 1901–1902* (London & Bombay: Longmans, Green, & Co, 1902).

Jamison, Kay Redfield. *Touched with Fire: Manic-Depressive Illness and the Artistic Temperament* (New York: Free Press, 1996).

Jung, C.G. On Psychic Energy (In *The Structure and Dynamics of the Psyche* (Collected Work of CG Jung), New York: Routledge, volume 8, 1970).

Jung, Carl Gustav. *Man and His Symbols* (New York: Doubleday hardcover, 1964).

Jung-Beeman M, et al. Neural Activity When People Solve Verbal Problems with Insight (*Biology*, 2, 2004), pp. 500–510.

Kandinsky, Wassily, Sadler, M.T. (Translator), & Glew, Adrian (Editor). *Concerning the Spiritual in Art* (New York: MFA Publications and London: Tate Publishing, 2001).

Koestler, Arthur. *The Act of Creation* (London, UK: Hutchinson & Co, 1964).

Korzybski, Alfred. *Collected Writings 1920–1950* (New York: Institute of General Semantics, 1990).

Korzybski, Alfred. *Science and Sanity: An Introduction to Non-Aristotelian Systems and General Semantics* (New York: Institute of General Semantics, 5th edition, 1994).

Kruglanski, A.W. & Gigerenzer, G. Intuitive and Deliberate Judgments Are Based on Common Principles (*Psychological Review*, 118(1), January 2011), pp. 97–109.

Kuhn, Thomas S. *The Structure of Scientific Revolutions* (Chicago, IL: University of Chicago Press, 1962).

Kuszewski, Andrea. *The Essential Psychopathology of Creativity*, 2010. https://ieet.org/index.php/IEET2/more/kuszewski20100928 (accessed 1 April 2021).

Kyaga, S., Lichtenstein, P., Boman, M., Hultman, C., Långström, N., & Landén, M. Creativity and Mental Disorder: Family Study of 300 000 People with Severe Mental Disorder (*The British Journal of Psychiatry*, 199(5), 2011), pp. 373–379.

Lakoff, George & Johnson, Mark. *Philosophy in the Flesh: The Embodied Mind and Its Challenge to Western Thought* (New York: Basic Books, 1999).

Lakoff, George & Johnson, Mark. *Metaphors We Live By* (Chicago, IL: University of Chicago Press, 1st edition, 2003).

Langley, P. Systematic and Nonsystematic Search Strategies (In J. Hendler, (Ed.), *Intelligence Planning Systems: Proceedings of the First International Conference*, San Francisco, CA: Morgan Kaufmann Pub, 1992), pp. 145–152.

Langley, P. & Jones, R. *A Computational Model of Scientific Insight* (In R.J. Sternberg, (Ed.), *The Nature of Creativity: Contemporary Psychological Perspectives*, Cambridge: Cambridge University Press, 1988).

Lautman, Albert. *Mathematics, Ideas, and the Physical Real* (*Mathématiques, les idées et le réel physique*, 1938, translated by Simon B. Duffy, New York: Continuum International Publishing Group, 2011).

Library of Congress. *Rome Reborn: The Vatican Library & Renaissance Culture* https://www.loc.gov/exhibits/vatican/humanism.html (accessed 1 April 2021).

Lubart, T.I. Creativity (In R.J. Sternberg (Ed.), *Thinking and Problem Solving*, San Diego, CA: Academic, 1994), pp. 290–332.

Malinowski, Bronisław. *Magic, Science and Religion and Other Essays* (Glencoe, IL: The Free Press, 1948).

Månsson, Lena. Religiösa visioner och mystik erfarenhet (*Tidningen Kulturen*, 9 februari, 2009).

Maslow, Arthur. *Toward a Psychology of Being* (New York: Wiley, 1962).

Mathers, Colin D., Ezzati, Majid, Jamison, Dean T. & Myrray, Christopher J.L. *Global Burden of Disease and Risk Factors* (New York: Oxford University Press and The World Bank, 2006).

McGinn, Bernard. Mystical Union in Judaism, Christianity and Islam (In Lindsay Jones (Ed.), *MacMillan Encyclopedia of Religion*, New York: MacMillan, 2005).

Mental Health Information. *Schizophrenia*. https://www.nimh.nih.gov/health/topics/schizophrenia/index.shtml#part_145430 (accessed 1 April 2021).

Miller, G.A. The Cognitive Revolution: A Historical Perspective (*Trends in Cognitive Sciences*, 7(3), 2003), pp. 141–144.

Mondin, Battista. Tillich's Doctrine of Religious Symbolism (*The Principle of Analogy in Protestant and Catholic Theology*, New York: Springer, 1963), pp. 118–146.

Nelson, B. & Rawlings, D. Relating Schizotypy and Personality to the Phenomenology of Creativity (*Schizophrenia Research*, 36, 2010), pp. 388–399.

Nettle, Daniel. An Evolutionary Approach to the Extraversion Continuum (*Evolution and Human Behavior*, 26(4), July 2005), pp. 363–373.

Neumann, Erich. *Art and the Creative Unconscious* (Princeton, NJ: Princeton University Press, 1974 edition).

Neus, Barrantes Vidal. *Creativity & Madness Revisited from Current Psychological Perspectives* (*Journal of Consciousness Studies*, 11(3–4), January 2004), pp. 58–78.

Niu, Weihua & Sternberg, Robert J. The Philosophical Roots of Western and Eastern Conceptions of Creativity (*Journal of Theoretical and Philosophical Psychology*, 26(1–2), 2006), pp. 18–38.

Ochse, R. *Before the Gates of Excellence: The Determinants of Creative Genius* (New York: Cambridge University Press, 1990).

Ogden, Charles Kay & Richards, Ivor A. *The Meaning of Meaning: A Study of the Influence of Language upon Thought and of the Science of Symbolism* (Eastford, CT: Martino Fine Book, 2013, original 1923).

Öllinger, Michael, Volz, Kirsten & Szathmáry, Eörs. Insight and Intuition – Two Sides of the Same Coin? (*Frontiers in Psychology*, 9, 2018), p. 689.

Öllinger, Michael & von Müller, Albrecht. Search and Coherence-Building in Intuition and Insight Problem Solving (*Frontiers in Psychology*, 8, 2017), p. 827.

Orrell, David. *Truth or Beauty: Science and the Quest for Order* (New Haven: Yale University Press, 2012).

Otto, Rudolf. *The Idea of the Holy, An Inquiry into the Non-Rational Factor in the Idea of the Divine and its Relation to the Rational* (Transl. of Das Heilige, Oxford: Oxford University Press, 1923).

Paden, William E. Comparative Religion (In John Hinnells (Ed.), *The Routledge Companion to the Study of Religion*, Philadelphia, PA: Routledge, 2009).

Parker, G. (Ed.). *Bipolar II Disorder: Modeling, Measuring and Managing* (Cambridge: Cambridge University Press, 2005).

Perruchet, P., Gallego, J., Savy, I. A Critical Reappraisal of the Evidence for Unconscious Abstraction of Deterministic Rules in Complex Experimental Situations (*Cognitive Psychology*, 22(4), October 1990), pp. 493–516.

Plato. *The Republic of Plato Vol. 2 Books VI-X* (Cambridge Library Collection – Classics, Cambridge: Cambridge University Press, Reissue edition, 2010).

Poincaré, Henri. Mathematical Creation (*The Monist*, XX, 1910), pp. 321–335.

Popper, Karl. *Objective Knowledge: An Evolutionary Approach* (Oxford: Oxford University Press, 1972).

Ritter, S.M. & Dijksterhuis, A. Creativity-The Unconscious Foundations of the Incubation Period (*Frontiers in Human Neuroscience*, 8, 2014), p. 215.

Rothenberg, Albert, Hausman, Carl R., & Durham, N. *The Creativity Question* (Durham, NC: Duke University Press Books, 1976).

Runco, M.A. Divergent Thinking, Creativity, and Ideation (In J.C. Kaufman & R.J. Sternberg (Eds.), *The Cambridge Handbook of Creativity*, New York: Cambridge University Press, 2010), pp. 413–446.

Runco, M.A. *Creativity and Reason in Cognitive Development* (Cambridge: Cambridge University Press, 2006).

Sass, Louis, A. *Madness and Modernism: Insanity in the Light of Modern Art, Literature, and Thought* (New York: Basic Books, 1st edition, 1992).

Schmidhuber, Joergen. Developmental Robotics, Optimal Artificial Curiosity, Creativity, Music, and the Fine Arts (*Connection Science*, 18(2), 2006), pp. 173–187.

Schwáb, Zoltán. Mind the Gap: The Impact of Wolfgang Iser's Reader-Response Criticism on Biblical Studies--A Critical Assessment (*Literature & Theology*, 17(2), Literary Hermeneutics, June 2003), p. 170.

Segal, David. *Just Manic Enough: Seeking Perfect Entrepreneurs* (New York Times, 18 September 2018).

Segal, E. Incubation in Insight Problem Solving (*Creativity Research Journal*, 16(1), 2004), pp. 141–148.

Simonton, Dean Keith. Creativity as Blind Variation and Selective Retention: Is the Creative Process Darwinian? (*Psychological Inquiry*, 10(4), 1999), pp. 309–328.

Sio, U.N. & Ormerod, T.C. Does Incubation Enhance Problem Solving? A Meta-Analytic Review (*Psychological Bulletin*, 135(1), January 2009), pp. 94–120.

Sircello, Guy. *A New Theory of Beauty. Princeton Essays on the Arts*, 1 (Princeton, NJ: Princeton University Press, 1975).

Smith, S.M. & Dodds, R.A. Incubation (In M.A. Runco & S.R. Pritzker (Eds.), *Encyclopedia of Creativity*, San Diego, CA: Academic Press, 1999), pp. 39–43.

Sternberg, R.J. A Triangular Theory of Love (*Psychological Review*, 93, 1986), pp. 119–135.

Sternberg, R.J., & Lubart, T.I. Investing in Creativity (*American Psychologist*, 51(7), 1996), pp. 677–688.

Sulloway, F.J. *Born to Rebel: Birth Order, Family Dynamics, and Creative Lives* (New York: Pantheon Books, 1996).

Taylor, John R. *Cognitive Grammar* (Oxford: Oxford University Press, 2002).

Tillich, Paul J. *Dynamics of Faith* (New York: Harper & Row, 1957).

Topolinski, Sascha & Strack, Fritz. The Analysis of Intuition: Processing Fluency and Affect in Judgments of Semantic Coherence (*Cognition and Emotion*, 23(8), December 2009), pp. 1465–1503.

Veale, T. & Donoghue, D.O. Computation and Blending (*Cognitive Linguistics*, 11(3–4), 2000), pp. 253–282.

Wallas, Graham. *The Art of Thought* (Kent, England: Solis Press; 2014 edition, original 1926).

Wertheimer, Max. *Productive Thinking* (New York: Harper, 1945).

Wright Buckham, John. The Mysticism of Plato (*The Open Court*, 1923(8), 1923), Article 2.

INDEX

abstraction 27, 64, 80, 81, 82, 83
academic fields 78–79
The Act of Creation (Koestler) 57
adaptation, compensatory 32
Adler, A. 21
algorithm 71
anthropometer 82
anxiety 9, 31, 54
Arieti, S. 53
Aristotle 30
art 20, 41–47, 57–59
Art and The Creative Unconscious
   (Neumann) 45
artificial intelligence (AI) 2, 65,
   70–74, 76, 82, 84, 86
artists 7, 32, 42–46
The Art of Thought (Wallas) 8
automatisation 27, 54–55

Bassler, J.: *The Parable of the Loaves* 49
Batson, C.D. 53, 54

bipolar disorder 31, 33
bisociation 57–59, 61–63, 75
blending process
   blend space 75
   cross-space mapping 75
   generic space 75
   knowledge spaces 75
blend space 75
Boden, M.A. 11
Bohm, D. 56–57; *On Creativity* 62
Bohr, N. 57

chaos 9, 50, 55, 63
cognition 35, 54, 62, 64
cognitive process 12, 62
   primary 53
   secondary 53
   tertiary 53
combinatorial thinking 35
communication 63
compensatory adaptation 32

computational creativity
69–87
conceptual abstractions 64
conceptual blending 75, 76,
79, 85
Concerning the spiritual in art
(Kandinsky) 43
conscious 9, 23, 26–28, 46, 51,
60, 61
convergent thinking 14
creative breakthroughs 23, 60,
62, 70
creative solution 12, 26,
71, 82
abstractions 27
automatisation 27
bounded rationality 27
false assumptions 27
functional fixations 27
opportunistic assimilation 27
remote association 28
schemata 28
creative value-adding ideas
area 13
expertise 13
individual 13
creativity 5
art 41–47
combinational 11
computational 69–87
and conscious 26–28
defined 10
and dishonesty 11
domain expertise 6–7
economy 58

emphasis 58
essence of 57
exploratory 11
flow 13
historical perspective 7–8
incubation 21–23
integrated 21
linguistics 56–64
literature 56–64
and madness 30–35
mysticism 47–55
originality 58
preparation 9
primary 11, 20
secondary 11, 20–21
stages of 8–10
illumination 9–10
incubation 9
preparation 9
verification 10
thinking 14
transformational 11–12
and unconscious 23–26
cross-space mapping 75
Csíkszentmihályi, M. 13
cultural stereotypes 64
cultures 43, 46, 54, 86

de-automatisation 54–55
decision-making process
22, 47
Deikman, A.J. 52
delusions 31, 32
depression 31
descriptive words 80

displacement defence
    mechanism 45
divergent thinking 14
divine force 3, 8, 47, 49

EII *see* explicit-implicit interac-
    tion theory (EII)
Einstein, A. 5, 10, 24–26, 47, 64
emotional stress 9
The Essential Psychopathology of Crea-
    tivity (Kuszewski) 33
explicit-implicit interaction
    theory (EII)
    abductive reasoning 30
    explicit knowledge 28–30
    implicit knowledge 29–30
    principles 28–30
    redundancy 29–30
explicit knowledge 28–30

The Fibonacci Patterns 44
flow 13

generalisation 22, 64, 80, 81
general semantics 80
generic space 75
geometric forms 44
Gimello, R.M. 52

hallucinations 31, 32
Hayakawa, S.I. 81
"hierarchy of needs" 20
human intelligence 72, 73
hypomania 34, 35
The Idea of the Holy (Otto) 51

imagination 8, 12, 61, 72, 73
implicit knowledge 28–30
incubation 9, 19, 21–24, 26,
    69, 73
inferential words 80
insights 5–7, 21–23, 43, 47, 53,
    69
integrated creativity 21
intuition 21–22, 43, 47, 69
Iser, W. 50

James, W. 52; *The Varieties of Reli-*
    gious Experience 51
Jung, C.G. 21, 42, 51

Kandinsky, W. 44; *Concerning the*
    spiritual in art 43
Knight's Move thinking 33
knowledge 19
    blending of 75–76
    domains 78–79
    explicit 28–30
    implicit 28–30
    spaces 75–77
Koestler, A. 57–61, 63, 70, 75,
    86; *The Act of Creation* 57
Korzybski, A. 80–84
Kuhn, T. 20; *The Structure of Scientific*
    Revolutions 19
Kuszewski, A.: *The Essential Psycho-*
    pathology of Creativity 33

labelled bisociation 70
language 25, 45, 48, 56, 63, 80,
    81

lateral thinking 14
Lautman, A. 57
Law of Contact or Contagion 56
Law of Similarity 56
linguistics 56–64, 70
literature 56–64, 70

machine learning 65, 82, 84
madness 14, 30–35
Madness and Modernism (Sass) 32
magic language 56, 62
Malevich, K. 44
Malinowski, B. 56
The Mandelbrot Fractals 44
mania 33–35
manic depression *see* bipolar
    disorder
Maslow, A. 20–21
mathematical patterns 44
matrices of thought 57,
    58, 62
melancholy 30
memes 13
mental ailments 31, 32
mental illnesses 31, 34, 53
metaphoric reasoning 63
metaphors 48, 49, 56, 62,
    63, 75
mood-creativity research 31
mysterium fascinans 51
mysterium tremendum 51
mystical experience 48, 49, 70
    characteristics 52
    features 52
mysticism 8, 47–55

Neumann, E. 46; *Art and The Crea-
    tive Unconscious* 45
Newton, I. 5
normality 30, 31, 42
numinous 51

Occam's razor principle 58
Ogden, C.K. 56
On Creativity (Bohm) 62
Otto, R.: *The Idea of the Holy* 51
overstimulation 55

The Parable of the Loaves (Bassler) 49
paranoia 31
Picasso, P. 11
Plato 7, 51
Poincaré, H. 24, 26, 79
Popper, K. 47
primary creativity 11, 20

rational thoughts 7, 26, 48, 51,
    58, 60
religious experience 53, 54, 62
religious mysticism 47–55
religious symbolism 49, 50
renaissance 8
Richards, I.A. 56

Sass, L.A.: *Madness and Modernism* 32
schizophrenia 31–33, 35
schizotypy 32
scientific breakthroughs 48, 58,
    73
scientific knowledge 19
secondary creativity 11, 20–21

secular art 41
self-actualisation 20
sensory input 55
silent presuppositions 80, 81, 82
Smith, G. 42
spiritual reality 43
spiritual world 43, 44
The Structure of Scientific Revolutions (Kuhn) 19
substance abuse 31
suprematism 44
surrealism 45
symbolic language 48, 49, 63
symbols 46, 49–51, 56

Tengberg, V. 42
thinking, creative
    abstract 63
    associative-based 15, 35, 64, 73
    convergent 14
    divergent 14
    Knight's Move 33
    lateral 14
Tillich, P. 49
trial-and-error process 47, 75

unconscious 9, 23–26, 45, 51, 61, 64, 69, 77, 82
under-stimulation 55
unio mystica 48
unipolar depression 31
unspoken phenomenon 42, 45, 56, 59, 69, 77, 82, 86

The Varieties of Religious Experience (James) 51
Ventis, W.L. 53, 54
verbal articulations 84
da Vinci, L. 8

Wallas, G. 3, 8–10, 20, 53, 55, 60, 61, 69; *The Art of Thought* 8
West, L.J. 55

Printed in the United States
by Baker & Taylor Publisher Services